Up & Running
with Harvard Graphics

Up & Running
with Harvard™ Graphics

Rebecca Bridges Altman

SYBEX®

San Francisco • Paris • Düsseldorf • Soest

Acquisitions Editor: Dianne King
Series Editor: Joanne Cuthbertson
Editor: Carol Henry
Technical Editor: Dan Tauber
Word Processors: Paul Erickson, Lisa Mitchell
Book Designer: Elke Hermanowski
Icon Designer: Helen Bruno
Screen Graphics: Cuong Le
Desktop Production Artist: Charlotte Carter
Proofreader: M. D. Barrera
Indexer: Ted Laux
Cover Designer: Archer Designs
Screen reproductions produced by XenoFont.

XenoFont is a trademark of XenoSoft.

SYBEX is a registered trademark of SYBEX, Inc.

TRADEMARKS: SYBEX has attempted throughout this book to distinguish proprietary trademarks from descriptive terms by following the capitalization style used by the manufacturer.

SYBEX is not affiliated with any manufacturer.

Every effort has been made to supply complete and accurate information. However, SYBEX assumes no responsibility for its use, nor for any infringement of the intellectual property rights of third parties which would result from such use.

Library of Congress Card Number: 90-71219
ISBN: 0-89588-736-3

Manufactured in the United States of America
10 9 8 7 6 5 4 3 2 1

Acknowledgments

I would first like to thank one of my clients, Oral-B Laboratories. The MIS department (in particular, Jim Sawyer and Ofelia Hopson) encouraged me to learn Harvard Graphics several years ago so that I could teach Oral-B employees how to use their company's standard graphics package. By teaching Harvard Graphics and helping people create their charts for presentations (and troubleshooting the inevitable problems along the way), I gained the experience necessary to write this book.

Secondly, I would like to thank my sister-in-law, Jody Altman, for her help in designing the charts for the employee presentation example used throughout the book. Her expertise in human resources was invaluable.

Rebecca Bridges Altman
October 1990

SYBEX
Up & Running Books

The Up & Running series of books from SYBEX has been developed for committed, eager PC users who would like to become familiar with a wide variety of programs and operations as quickly as possible. We assume that you are comfortable with your PC and that you know the basic functions of word processing, spreadsheets, and database management. With this background, Up & Running books will show you in 20 steps what particular products can do, and how to use them.

Who this book is for

Up & Running books are designed to save you time and money. First, you can avoid purchase mistakes by previewing products before you buy them—exploring their features, strengths, and limitations. Second, once you decide to purchase a product, you can learn its basics quickly by following the 20 steps—even if you are a beginner.

What this book provides

The first step always covers software installation in relation to hardware requirements. You'll learn whether the program can operate with your available hardware as well as various methods for starting the program. The second step introduces the program's user interface. The remaining 18 steps demonstrate the program's basic functions, using examples and short descriptions.

Contents and structure

 A clock shows the amount of time you can expect to spend at your computer for each step. Naturally, you'll need much less time if you only read through the step rather than complete it at your computer.

Special symbols and notes

You can also focus on particular points by scanning the short notes in the margins and locating the sections you are most interested in.

Symbols

In addition, three symbols highlight particular sections of text:

 The Action symbol highlights important steps that you will carry out.

 The Tip symbol indicates a practical hint or special technique.

 The Warning symbol alerts you to a potential problem and suggestions for avoiding it.

We welcome your comments

We have structured the Up & Running books so that the busy user spends little time studying documentation and is not burdened with unnecessary text. An Up & Running book cannot, of course, replace a lengthier book that contains advanced applications. However, you will get the information you need to put the program to practical use and to learn its basic functions in the shortest possible time.

SYBEX is very interested in your reactions to the Up & Running series. Your opinions and suggestions will help all of our readers, including yourself. Please send your comments to: SYBEX Editorial Department, 2021 Challenger Drive, Alameda, CA 94501.

Preface

Harvard Graphics is currently the most popular graphics package available for IBM personal computers and compatibles. Its stable position at the top of the best-seller charts is well earned. First of all, the program produces professional-looking charts, suitable for even the most formal of presentations. Secondly, Harvard offers options for almost every single aspect of the chart, allowing you to use all of your creativity in designing your charts. You can further enhance a chart by adding text, geometric lines and shapes, and clip art to any area of the chart. Another reason for Harvard Graphics' success is its ability to import data from spreadsheet programs like Lotus 1-2-3.

Although this book is based on the latest version of Harvard Graphics, version 2.3, users of previous versions will also find the book helpful. (Features new to 2.3 are clearly indicated throughout the book.)

Every powerful program, including Harvard Graphics, requires training and practice—that's where this book enters the picture. *Up & Running with Harvard Graphics* covers all the major features of the program, with enough detail to get you—you guessed it—up and running.

Table of Contents

Step 1

Installation

Your first step is to install the Harvard Graphics program on your computer, using the easy-to-follow INSTALL program. Once the software is copied to your hard disk, you need to start Harvard Graphics and change the defaults to match your hardware configuration. These procedures are outlined in Step 1.

Hardware Requirements

Harvard Graphics version 2.3 requires the following hardware:

- 6.5Mb of available hard disk space, or 3Mb if you don't install the Sample, Symbols, and Tutorial files.

- A minimum of 512K RAM. If you are using the MACRO program, Online Tutorial, a network, or a VDI (Virtual Device Interface) device, you need a minimum of 640K. (A VDI is required for certain printers and film recorders, and to create metafiles.)

- DOS 2.1 or later.

- A graphics adapter.

Of course, you will need a printer or plotter to produce hardcopy output. A mouse is optional.

Using the INSTALL Program

Although installation is not fast, it couldn't be easier. The INSTALL program leads you through the entire process. It asks you where you want to install the program (C:\HG is the default drive and directory) and then copies each disk to the specified directory. You are prompted to change disks when necessary.

Follow these steps to begin the INSTALL program.

1.   Insert Harvard Graphics Disk 1 in drive A.

2.   Type

   A:

   and press Enter to go to drive A.

3.   Type

   INSTALL

   and press Enter.

4.   Read the message about installation and press any key.

5.   When prompted, specify the drive and subdirectory for Harvard Graphics.

Determin-
ing which
files to
copy

You next see the INSTALL Main Menu. Give careful considera-
tion to which files you want to install. If you select *All files except
VDI devices,* you must have 6.5Mb of disk space available and up
to an hour of free time. If you are short on time and/or disk space,
choose *Program files only.* You can always come back to this
menu later and install other files. Because you are using this book
to learn Harvard Graphics, you probably won't need the Tutorial
or Sample files. The Symbols files contain over 500 clip-art pictures you can use in your charts.

If you want to install just the Program and Symbols files, first
choose *Program files only.* Once these files are copied, you are
returned to the INSTALL main menu. You can then choose
Symbols only.

6.   Highlight your file installation selection on the INSTALL
     main menu (Figure 1.1) and press Enter.

7.   Highlight your country abbreviation and press Enter.

```
                    ↑ ↓, Press ↵ to continue

              ┌──────────────────────────────────┐
              │ Install Harvard Graphics Main Menu │
              │                                    │
              │  ► All files except UDI devices    │
              │    Program files only              │
              │    Tutorial only                   │
              │    Sample files only               │
              │    Symbols only                    │
              │    UDI device files                │
              │    Exit                            │
              └──────────────────────────────────┘

       If you're new to Harvard Graphics, choose "All files except
       UDI devices".  If you're familiar with Harvard Graphics or
       if you have less than 6.5 MB of space available on your hard
       drive, install only the files you need.
```

Figure 1.1: INSTALL program main menu

8. When prompted, insert the indicated disks.

9. When the INSTALL main menu reappears, choose another option to copy additional files, or choose Exit.

Starting Harvard Graphics

Loading Harvard Graphics is like loading your other software programs. You need to change to the directory where the program resides, and then type the command to load the program.

Follow these steps to load Harvard Graphics:

1. Change to the Harvard Graphics directory. For example, at your DOS prompt, type

   CD \HG

   and press Enter.

2. Type

   HG

and press Enter to start the program. You will see the Harvard Graphics Main Menu. This menu is explained in Step 2.

Mouse installation

If you want to use your mouse with Harvard Graphics, you need to load your mouse software before you start Harvard. Refer to your mouse documentation for details.

Configuring Harvard Graphics

I'm sure you are anxious to start creating charts, but you must do a bit more preparation work before you get to the "good stuff." You need to check the setup defaults to make sure they are appropriate for your computer system. Option 9, *Setup*, on Harvard's Main Menu is where you specify your hardware configuration.

Setting Up the Screen

Graphics adapters

Harvard Graphics makes its best guess as to what type of graphics adapter you have (for example, CGA, VGA, or Hercules), but you should double-check this setting.

Follow these steps to specify your graphics adapter:

1. On the Main Menu, type **9** to choose *Setup*.

2. On the Setup menu, type **6** to choose *Screen*. A two-column list of adapters is displayed.

3. Press the spacebar until your screen type is highlighted.

4. Press F10 to confirm your selection.

Menu colors

Now specify the color scheme for your menus. You can choose from three different color combinations, or choose monochrome if you don't have a color monitor or if you prefer a single color.

Follow these steps to choose your menu colors:

1. On the Setup menu, type **1** to choose *Defaults*. A screen displays the current default settings for the program. Most

of these defaults will be discussed at relevant points throughout the book.

2.   Press End to go to the last option on this screen, *Menu colors*.

The pointer indicates the current color scheme. If you do not have a color monitor, you should select *Monochrome*. Otherwise, try the different color schemes and find the one you prefer.

3.   Press the spacebar to move the pointer to a different color scheme.

4.   Press F10 to confirm your selection.

Selecting Output Devices

Harvard Graphics lets you produce your charts on three types of output devices: printers, plotters, and film recorders (for 35-mm slides). The options for specifying output devices are on the Setup menu. You can configure Harvard Graphics for two different printers.

This exercise takes you through the steps for installing your printer.

Installing a printer

1.   On the Setup menu, type **2** to choose *Printer 1*. A screen of printer choices appears.

2.   Use the arrow keys or spacebar to highlight your printer.

3.   Press F10 to confirm your selection.

4.   In the dialog box that next appears, choose your printer port. Most printers use parallel port LPT1. If yours does, proceed to step 7.

5.   If you use a different parallel port (LPT2 or LPT3), or a serial port (COM1 or COM2), use the spacebar to select the appropriate port.

6. If necessary, change the serial port information (baud rate, parity, data bits, and stop bits).

7. Press F10.

8. Press Esc to return to the Main Menu.

Step 2

The User Interface

A *user interface* lets you interact with a software program. In Harvard Graphics, you give commands by choosing options from menus and by pressing function and control keys. Step 2 explains these various techniques.

Menus

When you start Harvard Graphics, the menu shown in Figure 2.1 appears. Table 2.1 explains each of the options on the Main Menu. Harvard Graphics offers several ways to choose menu options. First, you can type the highlighted number to the right of the menu item. For example, you can type **2** to choose *Enter/Edit chart*. Alternatively, you can use the spacebar or the up and down arrow keys to highlight an option, and press Enter. Or, if you have a mouse, you can glide the mouse up or down to highlight the option and then click the left mouse button.

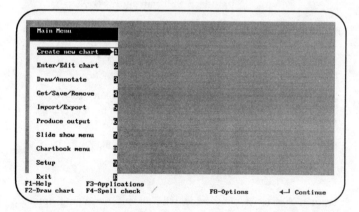

Figure 2.1: The Harvard Graphics Main Menu

Option	Action
Create new chart	Specify a chart type and begin designing a new chart.
Enter/Edit chart	Work on the current chart. You can modify data, specify special options, or format the appearance of the current chart.
Draw/Annotate	Access the Draw program, which lets you type text and create shapes anywhere on the chart. See Steps 14 and 15.
Get/Save/Remove	Manipulate Harvard Graphics files. Lets you retrieve an existing chart, save the current chart, or delete charts you no longer need. See Step 4.
Import/Export	Bring in data and graphs from other programs, such as Lotus 1-2-3, or prepare them for use by other programs. See Steps 18 and 19.
Produce output	Print a chart on a printer or plotter, or produce a 35-mm slide. See Step 6.
Slide show menu	Create a computer-driven slide show of your charts. Also used to batch-print a series of charts. See Step 13.
Chartbook menu	Organize templates. See Step 17.
Setup	Configure Harvard Graphics for your printer and screen. Also used to change default settings. See Step 1.
Exit	Quit Harvard Graphics and go to DOS.

Table 2.1: Main Menu Option

Escaping from a menu

It's not a disaster if you accidentally choose the wrong option: Simply press Esc or click the right mouse button to return to the Main Menu.

Many of the options on the Main Menu display submenus. For in-stance, when you choose option 1, *Create new chart,* a submenu lists the types of charts you can create. You select options from submenus the same way you do from the Main Menu.

To get acquainted with the Harvard Graphics interface, let's create a pie chart. (You won't actually be creating the chart—just choosing the menu options to create this chart type.)

1. From the Main Menu, choose option **1**, *Create new chart.* Notice that the Main Menu remains on the screen and the submenu appears to its right. So that you can see the path of your menu options, Harvard Graphics displays each menu that you have selected.

2. Select option **2**, *Pie.* The pie chart data form appears. This is where you will eventually enter the specifics of how you want your pie chart to look.

3. For now, just examine the data form, and then press Esc to return to the Main Menu.

Function Keys

Some of Harvard's commands are accessed through the function keys on your keyboard. Whenever function keys are available, you will see them listed at the bottom of the screen. As you can see on the Main Menu, the following function keys are now available:

- F1 displays a Help screen
- F2 draws the current chart
- F3 displays a list of other applications you can load
- F4 spell-checks the current chart
- F7 changes the size and position of the chart on the page
- F8 lists current chart options (orientation, fonts, borders)

You will find that Harvard Graphics uses function keys consistently throughout the program. For example, when you are creating or modifying a chart,

- F1 is your Help key
- F2 draws the chart
- F3 saves the chart
- F4 brings the chart into the Draw/Annotate screen
- F5 assigns text attributes (like bold or italic)
- F7 changes the size and placement of text
- F8 displays chart options
- F10 continues to the next step or executes the command

However, you don't need to memorize these keys—they are always listed at the bottom of the screen when they are available.

You can also choose function keys with the mouse. First, press the left and right buttons simultaneously. The first function, F1-Help, is highlighted. Now you can use the mouse to highlight the desired function at the bottom of the screen, and then click the left button.

Follow these steps to practice using some of the function keys:

1. From the Main Menu, press F1 to view a Help screen.
2. Read the Help screen.
3. As the bottom of the screen indicates, press Esc to cancel the Help screen. The Main Menu reappears.
4. Press F8 to view the current chart options. (You will learn about these options later.)
5. Press Esc to return to the Main Menu.

Entering Data

When you create a chart, Harvard Graphics displays a screen into which you enter data (text and/or numbers). This screen is called the *chart data form;* you saw one earlier when you selected *Pie* on the Create New Chart menu. The layout of the form varies depending on the type of chart you are creating. Regardless of the chart type, you follow these general rules to position the cursor for data entry:

- Use the Enter key to move the cursor to the beginning of the next line.
- Use the Tab key to move to the beginning the next column.
- If the line doesn't have another column, the Tab key moves to the beginning of the next line.
- Press Shift-Tab to move to the beginning of the previous column.

Moving the cursor in the data form

You may also use the arrow keys to move the cursor a character at a time in the direction of the arrow. However, since you usually want to move the cursor to the beginning of a line or column, it's faster to use Enter and Tab.

Mouse users can position the cursor with the mouse. Just slowly move the mouse around your desktop to move the cursor in the direction you want.

Using the mouse on the data form

Follow these steps to practice moving the cursor:

1. From the Main Menu, choose option **2,** *Enter/Edit chart.* The pie chart data form is displayed. At this stage, don't worry about what everything on your screen means. The point of this exercise is to practice moving the cursor around the screen.

2. Press Enter to move from line to line until the cursor is in the Label column, next to Slice 1.

3. Press Tab to move from column to column.

4. Press Shift-Tab to move to the previous column.

5. Press Esc or F10 to return to the Main Menu.

Choosing Options

Whenever Harvard Graphics offers several options, you will see a marker next to the current option. Figure 2.2 displays the Current Chart Options screen that you get when you press F8 on the Main Menu. Notice the pointers next to *Landscape, None,* and *Executive.*

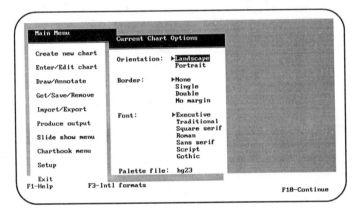

Figure 2.2: The pointers indicate the current chart options

Moving the options pointer

To choose a different option, you need to move the pointer next to the option you want. Harvard Graphics offers several ways to move the pointer. Take your pick.

- Press the spacebar until the pointer is next to the desired option.

- Use an arrow key to highlight an option, and then press the spacebar.

- Use an arrow key to highlight an option, and then press Enter. The marker points at the option, *and* the cursor moves down to the next block of options.

- Highlight an option with the mouse, and click the left button.

It really doesn't matter which technique you use; it's a matter of personal preference. Your author, a Harvard Graphics veteran, prefers the first method.

Practice choosing some options.

1. From the Main Menu, press F8 to display the Current Chart Options screen. You can change the chart's orientation, print a border around the chart, and specify the chart's font.

2. Press the spacebar until the pointer is next to *Portrait.*

3. Press Enter to select *Portrait* and move down to the next set of options *(Border).*

4. Press the spacebar until the pointer is next to *Single.* This option places a box around the chart.

5. Press Enter to select *Single* and move down to the next set of options *(Font).*

6. Choose *Roman,* using the pointer movement method of your choice.

7. The last option, *Palette file,* lets you use a different set of colors with the current chart. Color palettes are discussed in Step 20. Leave the palette at its current setting, and press F10 to return to the Main Menu.

Speed Keys

Another, faster way to issue commands in Harvard Graphics is with *speed keys.* For example, Ctrl-S saves the current chart. These speed-key commands are summarized in Table 2.2.

Speed Key	Action
Ctrl-D	Go to Draw Partner
Ctrl-G	Get a chart
Ctrl-L	Import Lotus 1-2-3 data
Ctrl-P	Print a chart
Ctrl-R	Go to Draw/Annotate
Ctrl-S	Save a chart
Ctrl-X	Import Excel data

Table 2.2: Speed Keys

The charts you will be creating in this book are for a presentation for the new employees of a fictitious toy manufacturing company called Tactile Toys. Ultimately, the charts will be made into overheads for the orientation program. In the process of preparing this presentation, you will learn all the chart types offered in Harvard Graphics.

In Step 3, you will learn the basic procedures for creating a chart. Although your first chart will be a text chart, many of the techniques you learn in this step apply to any chart type.

Choosing a Chart Type

Table 3.1 lists the chart types available in Harvard Graphics. This table gives a brief description of each chart. For a more thorough explanation, see the step that concentrates on the particular chart type.

Chart Type	Description
Text	Used for cover pages, lists, columnar tables.
Pie	Each pie slice represents a proportion of the total.
Bar	Bars are placed side by side to differentiate between the various data series. Optionally, bars can be stacked on top of one another.
Line	Data points are connected with lines to show a trend.
Organization	Shows the structure of a hierarchy, such as the positions of key people in a company.

Table 3.1: Chart Types

Chart Type	Description
Area	Similar to a line chart, except the area underneath the line is shaded.
High-Low-Close	Used primarily for illustrating stock data.

Table 3.1: Chart Types (continued)

Creating a title chart

Let's create a title chart, which is a type of text chart. Title charts are used as cover pages for reports or as introductory slides for a presentation. Follow these steps at your computer:

1. From the Main Menu, choose option **1**, *Create new chart.*

2. Choose option **1**, *Text,* and the Text submenu appears.

3. Choose option **1**, *Title chart.*

4. If you get the warning message "Latest changes have not been saved," press Enter to continue. You'll next see the chart data form.

The title chart contains three distinct areas, labeled Top, Middle, and Bottom. You can type up to three lines in each area.

Entering Chart Data

You will remember from Step 2 that you move the cursor to the next data-entry line by pressing Enter or Tab. To enter the titles in your chart, you simply place the cursor where you want to type the text and start typing. If you make a typing mistake, press the backspace key to back up and correct the error.

Follow the next set of steps to enter the data for your title chart example and then draw the chart on the screen.

1. Enter the titles shown in Figure 3.1.

2. Press F2 to draw the chart.

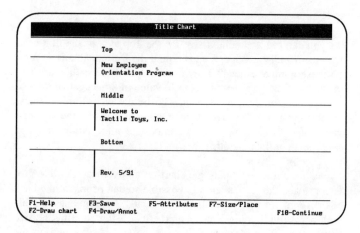

Figure 3.1: A title chart

No matter which type of chart you are creating, the Draw key (F2) uses your current data to draw the chart on the screen. This picture gives you a good representation of how the printed chart will look. Notice that each line in the title chart is centered, and that the titles in the top area are the largest. As you will soon see, you can change the size and placement of the text in your chart.

Drawing a chart

3. Press any key to return to the chart data form.

Changing the Size/Place

Harvard Graphics lets you change the size and placement of text in almost all chart types. The Size/Place key, F7, displays the size and placement choices in the left margin of the screen. (You were probably wondering what all that blank space was for!)

With the chart data form displayed, press F7. Notice in the window that appears at the left of the screen that you can change the size and placement of each line in each area (in other words, all nine lines).

Size

As you can see, the default size for the Top area of the title chart is 8, the Middle area's default is 6, and the Bottom area is 4. What do these numbers mean? They are *not* point sizes; they are percentages of the page length. Thus, a value of 8 means that the text is 8 percent of the page length. The best way to think of these numbers is as relative sizes. A size value of 4 is half the size of a value of 8. Make sure the most important information in a text chart is larger than the other text.

Truncated text

If you are going to display the chart on an overhead or slide projector, make the text as large as possible so that people at the back of the room are able to see the chart clearly. Experiment with different sizes until you get the desired effect. After entering the size value, press F2 to draw the chart. If the text is truncated on the screen, you have chosen too large a value.

Place

By default, all lines in a title chart are centered. The pointer next to the *C* on the Size/Place window indicates the line is centered on the page. If you change the placement to *L* or *R,* the text is aligned at the left or right margin.

Follow these steps to change the size and placement of your titles:

1. If the Size/Place options are not currently displayed, press F7.

2. To change the size of the first title, type **20** and press Enter.

3. Change the size of the second title, also, to **20.**

4. Press F2 to draw the chart. Notice that this larger size truncates the titles. You need to choose a different size.

5. Press any key.

6. Press the Size/Place key, F7.

7. Change the size of both the first two (Top) titles to **10.**

8. Increase the size of both the Middle titles to **8.**

9. Press F2 to redraw the chart. Now the titles fit comfortably on the page.

10. Press any key.

Follow these steps to right-align the Bottom title, "Rev. 5/91":

1. Press the Size/Place key, F7.

2. Press Enter until the cursor is on the same line as the title, "Rev. 5/91."

3. Press Tab to move the cursor to the Place column.

4. Press the spacebar to move the option pointer next to *R* (for Right).

5. Press F2 to draw the chart.

Changing the Attributes

Attributes define the text's character style. You can specify the following attributes for single characters or entire lines of text:

- Fill
- Bold
- Italic
- Underline
- Color

By default, the Fill and Bold attributes are turned on. Figure 3.2 illustrates text with and without the Fill and Bold attributes.

For presentation charts, do not turn off the default attributes, Fill and Bold. These attributes are the easiest to read on an overhead or slide.

Bold and Fill Turned On

Bold Turned On, Fill Turned Off

Fill Turned On, Bold Turned Off

Bold and Fill Turned Off

Figure 3.2: The Fill and Bold attributes

To change the attributes of chart text, you need to

- Position the cursor at the beginning of the text you want to format.

- Press the Attributes key, F5.

- Use the arrow keys to highlight the text you wish to format.

- Tab to the appropriate attribute at the bottom of the screen, and use the spacebar to toggle the pointer on or off.

- Press F10 to execute the Attributes command, or F2 to immediately view the chart.

When you want to format an entire line of text, press Shift-F5 instead of F5. The entire line will be highlighted automatically. To format additional lines below the current line, press the down arrow key.

Let's italicize the compnay name in your title chart; follow these steps:

1. Press any key to return to the chart data form.

2. Move the cursor to the beginning of the line "Tactile Toys."

3. Press the Attributes key, F5.

4. Press the right arrow key until the entire title is highlighted.

5. At the bottom of the screen, press Tab until the cursor is next to Italic.

6. Press the spacebar to select this attribute.

7. Press F2 to draw the chart. Notice the italicized title.

*Turning on
an attribute*

Now turn off the Bold attribute from the Bottom title, as follows:

1. Press any key.

2. Move the cursor to the line "Rev. 5/91."

3. Press Shift-F5. The entire line is highlighted automatically, and the Attributes menu appears at the bottom of the screen.

4. Press Tab until the cursor is next to Bold.

5. Press the spacebar to unmark the attribute.

6. Draw the chart.

*Turning off
an attribute*

7. Press Ctrl-S to save the chart.

8. Type the name **WELCOME** as the chart name and press F10. (You will learn more about saving in Step 4.)

9. Press Esc until the Main Menu is displayed.

Specifying Options

One of the most noteworthy benefits of Harvard Graphics is its abundance of options. Most of the chart types have at least one screen page of special options, and bar/line charts have four pages. For example, in a pie chart you can emphasize the slices with patterns, colors, or colored patterns. In a bar chart, you have options to choose a bar style (Cluster, Overlap, Stack, 100%, Step, or Paired). Harvard Graphics has an option for virtually every aspect of your chart.

When chart options are available, you will see F8-Options at the bottom of the screen. Press F8, and the top of the screen indicates

*Displaying
pages of
options*

the number of option pages. Figure 3.3 displays the first option page for a bar/line chart. Notice that the top of the screen says "Page 1 of 4." The PgDn key lets you display the next option page. To go back to the chart data form, press F8 again; this key toggles you between your data and the options.

```
┌──────────────────────────────────────────────────────────────┐
│         Bar/Line Chart   Titles & Options   Page 1 of 4        ▼│
│▲                                                               │
│            Title:                                              │
│            Subtitle:                                           │
│                                                                │
│            Footnote:                                           │
│                                                                │
│                                                                │
│          X  axis title:                                        │
│          Y1 axis title:                                        │
│          Y2 axis title:                                        │
│   Legend                        Type          Display │ Y Axis │
│   Title:            Bar  Line  Trend  Curve  Pt  Yes  No │ Y1  Y2│
│                                                                │
│   1 │ Series 1              Bar               Yes      │ Y1    │
│   2 │ Series 2              Bar               Yes      │ Y1    │
│   3 │ Series 3              Bar               Yes      │ Y1    │
│   4 │ Series 4              Bar               Yes      │ Y1    │
│   5 │ Series 5              Bar               Yes      │ Y1    │
│   6 │ Series 6              Bar               Yes      │ Y1    │
│   7 │ Series 7              Bar               Yes      │ Y1    │
│   8 │ Series 8              Bar               Yes      │ Y1    │
│                                                                │
│  F1-Help              F5-Attributes   F7-Size/Place            │
│  F2-Draw chart                        F8-Data       F10-Continue│
└──────────────────────────────────────────────────────────────┘
```

Figure 3.3: The first page of options for a bar/line chart

Chart Gallery

Another way to create a chart is with Release 2.3's new Chart Gallery feature. Using the Chart Gallery, you choose your chart type from on-screen examples. *From gallery* is option 8 on the Create New Chart menu. Instead of selecting *Pie* from a chart type list, you select a picture of a pie from the Gallery.

Saving time

The real value of the Chart Gallery, however, comes in the next step. After selecting the chart type, you see more examples of that particular chart type, each displaying different options. Figure 3.4 shows the gallery of bar charts. Once you choose one of these variations, the options for that particular chart style are automatically set for you. Beginners will appreciate this feature because

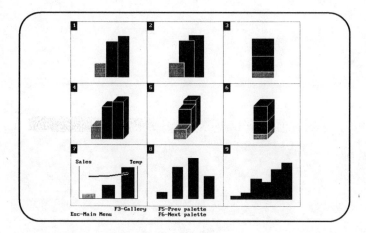

Figure 3.4: The bar chart gallery

they don't need to experiment with options, trying to achieve the look they want. Power users will enjoy the time saved by not having to manually set the options.

After selecting the Gallery chart type and style, the next step is to clear the sample data from the template. The F10 function key clears this data (but not the options) and takes you into the chart data form so that you can enter your own data.

Clearing sample data

Step 4

Storing and Retrieving Charts

File storage and management is an important part of using any software program. In the Main Menu, the *Get/Save/Remove* option is the gateway to file management in Harvard Graphics. Function keys and speed keys are also available for these tasks.

Saving Charts

Harvard Graphics offers three ways to save charts:

- From any chart data form, you can press F3.

- From the Main Menu or chart data form, you can press Ctrl-S.

- From the Main Menu, you can choose option 4, *Get/Save/ Remove,* and then option 2, *Save chart.*

The first time you save a file, you are prompted for both a name and a description. Use a maximum of eight characters; .CHT is automatically assigned as the extension. For the description, Harvard Graphics supplies your chart's title. You can accept this default, or enter your own description (up to 40 characters). Before you press F10 to execute the save, you should consider where you are storing the file.

Naming files

The top of the Save Chart dialog box indicates where the file will be saved (for example, in C:\HG). To save a file in a directory different from that shown, press Tab or Shift-Tab to move the cursor next to the Directory line. You can then edit or retype the path. Unfortunately, there is no way to display a directory list from the Save Chart dialog box. If you can't remember the correct directory name when you are saving a file, you must cancel the Save command and call up the Get Chart screen. This screen lets you navigate your directory structure when you press F3.

Saving in a different directory

*Changing
the default
directory*

If you find yourself always changing the directory when you save files, you should change your default directory. To specify a new default directory, you need to

- Choose option **9**, *Setup,* from the Main Menu.
- Choose option **1**, *Defaults.*
- Next to "Data directory," enter the complete path (for example, C:\HG\DATA).
- Press F10.

Getting a Chart

To retrieve a previously saved chart, you can use the *Get/Save/ Remove* option on the Main Menu or press the Ctrl-G speed key. Harvard Graphics then lists the file names in the current directory, along with the date each file was last modified, the chart type, and the description that you or Harvard Graphics assigned when you saved the file. With such detailed information, you can easily locate a particular file.

*Selecting
file names*

You can either type in the file name, or, if you see the file you want to retrieve, you can use the arrow keys to highlight its name and press Enter or F10. Mouse users can highlight the name and press the left mouse button. If you don't see your file name on the immediate screen, you can press PgDn to scroll through the list.

After you select a chart name, you will see either the chart or a message warning you that your latest changes have not been saved. When you see this message, you can choose to press Enter and thus discard the changes and retrieve the specified file. Or you can press Esc; this cancels the *Get chart* command so that you can save the edited file.

*Changing
directories*

If the file you want to load is located in a different subdirectory, you can use the F3 key to help you switch to the right directory.

Follow these steps to practice navigating your way around the directories on your hard disk:

1. From the Main Menu, choose option **4**, *Get/Save/Remove*.

2. Select option **1**, *Get chart*.

3. Press the F3 key to display the directories.

The first subdirectory on the list is the parent directory, indicated by two dots. This choice takes you to the previous level in the directory structure. The other entries on the list are subdirectories of the current directory. If you installed the complete Harvard Graphics program, the subdirectories listed in the \HG directory are SYMBOLS, GALLERY, and SAMPLE.

4. Highlight the GALLERY subdirectory and press Enter. Your screen now lists the files in the GALLERY directory.

5. To change to a different directory, press F3 again.

6. To go back to the parent directory (C:\HG), make sure the double dots are highlighted and press Enter.

7. Highlight any chart name and press Enter. The chart you selected is displayed on your screen.

8. Press any key, and the chart data form appears.

9. Press Esc to return to the Main Menu.

Removing a File

When you no longer need a chart, you should delete it so that it doesn't clutter up your hard disk. To delete a file, use the *Remove file* option on the Get/Save/Remove menu.

Remove file displays a screen of files identical to the one you see with the *Get chart* option. If you accidentally choose *Remove file* instead of *Get chart,* you can unintentionally delete a file. Fortunately, Harvard Graphics asks you to confirm your choice.

Going to DOS

If you are using Harvard Graphics, and you want to go to DOS temporarily to make a directory or back up your charts, you don't have to exit Harvard Graphics to enter DOS commands. Instead, use the Applications feature (Release 2.3 only). Once you have installed DOS on the Applications menu, you can easily "shell out" to DOS by

- Pressing F3 from the Main Menu
- Choosing the DOS option on the Applications menu

Adding an application

Follow these steps to add the DOS choice to your Applications menu:

1. From the Main Menu, choose option **9**, *Setup.*

2. Choose option **8**, *Applications.*

3. Press Tab until the cursor is next to an empty menu item (for example, *Menu item 3).*

4. Type

   `Go to DOS`

   and press Enter. This is the description that will appear on the Applications menu. You can type anything you like here.

5. Press Tab to move to *Command,* and type

   `command.com`

   This is the command that will be executed when you choose this option on the Applications menu.

6. Press F10 to save the new Applications menu item.

The DOS item is now permanently recorded in the Applications menu; you don't need to add it every time you want to use it.

7. From the Main Menu, press F3.

8. Choose *Go to DOS*. After a moment, your DOS prompt appears.

9. Type a DOS command, such as **DIR**.

10. To return to Harvard Graphics, type

    exit

    and press Enter. After a moment, the Harvard Graphics Main Menu appears.

Returning to Harvard Graphics

You can include up to eight different programs on the Applications menu. You may want to add your spreadsheet and word processing programs to the list. That way, you can go into these other programs and come back into Harvard Graphics, without having to reload Harvard Graphics. A sample Applications menu is shown in Figure 4.1; your own menu will display the programs you choose.

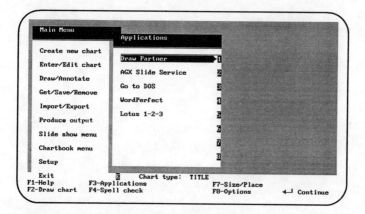

Figure 4.1 : A sample Applications menu

Harvard Graphics' text charts will help you illustrate key points and concepts in your presentation. You can create the following types of text charts:

- Title chart
- Simple list
- Bullet list
- Two columns
- Three columns
- Free-form

This step explains the unique capabilities of each chart type, and how to edit the text once you have created the chart. (The title chart has already been discussed in Step 3 and is not included here.)

If, after creating a chart, you realize the chart type you selected is not appropriate, you can easily transfer its data to a different chart type. Go back to the Main Menu and choose *Create new chart*. Select the text chart you want, and you will be asked if you want to "Keep current data." Press Enter to choose Yes.

Changing a chart type

Creating a Bullet List

The distinguishing feature of a bullet list is that it automatically includes bullets for each item in the list. This chart type is the fastest (though not the only) way to create a list of bulleted items.

Follow these steps to create the bullet list shown in Figure 5.1.

1. Choose option 1, *Create new chart*.
2. Choose option 1, *Text*.

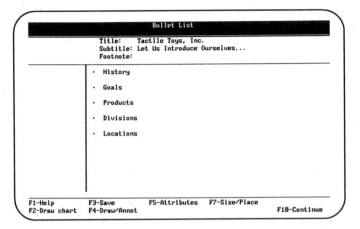

Figure 5.1: A bullet list

3. Choose option 3, *Bullet list*. If you get the "Keep current data." prompt, choose No. The chart data form appears.

4. Next to Title, type

    Tactile Toys, Inc.

    and press Enter.

5. Next to Subtitle, type

    Let Us Introduce Ourselves...

6. Press Enter until the cursor is in the main chart area. Notice that a round bullet automatically appears.

7. Type

    History

    and press Enter.

Inserting bullets

The cursor now moves down to the next line, staying aligned with the beginning of the text in the previous line. The list you are creating here does *not* have a second-level bullet. However, you could create a second level of bullets that are indented from the level you just entered. To do so, you would press Ctrl-B and select a bullet shape.

8. Press Enter to display the automatic bullet. Notice that the automatic bullet appeared because you double-spaced the text.

9. Use the chart data in Figure 5.1 to complete your bullet list. Be sure to double-space the list to get the automatic bullets.

10. Press F2 to display the chart.

Changing the Bullet Shape

The default bullet shape is a solid circle, but you can also use a dash, check mark, solid square, or Arabic numbers. To change the bullet shape, press the Size/Place key, F7.

Change the shape of the bullets in your text chart.

1. Press the Size/Place key, F7.

2. Press Enter to move under *Bullet Shape.*

3. Press the spacebar until the # sign is marked. This bullet type automatically numbers the items when you draw or print the chart.

4. Press F10. Notice that you do *not* see the numbers on the chart data form; you see # signs where the number will appear.

5. Press F2 to draw the chart. Each item is now numbered.

6. Change the bullet shape to a check mark.

7. Press F3 and save the chart with the name **OVERVIEW**.

Aligning the List

You may have noticed on the Size/Place screen that there are options for changing the size, placement, and indentation of the list.

The default placement is centered. This does not mean that each line is centered; rather, it means that the longest list item is in the center of the page. The other bullets are left-aligned with the one in the longest item.

Indenting the list

The *Indent* option on the Size/Place screen lets you slide the entire list to the right (when the list is left-aligned). The number you choose represents a percentage of the page width. For example, if you want the list to begin 20% of the way across the page, you would enter 20.

If the bulleted items are centered, and you want them pushed to the left, you should change the placement option to left (L) and set an indent.

Creating a Simple List

Although a simple list does not automatically contain bullets, this chart type is more flexible than the bullet list. The spacing in a bullet list is quite strict—double-spacing automatically gives you a bullet (whether you want one or not), and indented bullets cannot have a blank line above them. A simple list, in contrast, can have any kind of line spacing you want, and you can insert a bullet anywhere.

Follow these steps to create the simple list shown in Figure 5.2:

1. Create a simple list; do not keep the current data.
2. Enter the title and subtitle shown in Figure 5.2.
3. Press Enter until the cursor is in the main chart area.
4. Press Ctrl-B to insert a bullet.

Creating a bullet

5. Press the spacebar until the marker is pointing to the square bullet, and press Enter.

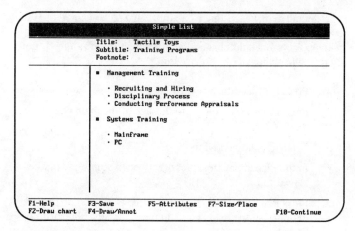

Figure 5.2: A simple list

6. Press the spacebar twice to add additional space after the bullet, and then type

   Management Training

   and press Enter twice.

7. Press the spacebar until the cursor is aligned with the *M* in "Management," and press Ctrl-B to insert a bullet.

8. Press the spacebar until the marker is pointing to the round bullet, and press Enter.

9. Press the spacebar to insert a space, and then type

   Recruiting and Hiring

   and press Enter. Notice that the cursor is automatically aligned with the bullet on the previous line.

10. Finish the chart as shown in Figure 5.2. Remember to press Ctrl-B to insert bullets.

11. Draw the chart with F2. Notice that each line is centered and the bullets do not line up.

The default is for each line in a simple list to be centered. However, this type of placement is not appropriate for a list containing bullets, so you should change the placement to left-aligned. Let's do this, and change the chart size, too.

*Changing
text size*

1. Press the Size/Place key, F7.

2. Press Enter until you get to the size of the main chart (currently 5.5).

3. Type **5.0**, and press Tab.

*Changing
text
alignment*

4. In the Placement area, press the spacebar until the marker is next to *L*.

5. Press F2 to draw the chart. Each line is aligned on the left margin, but the list is now too far to the left; it needs to be indented.

*Indenting
a list*

6. Press F7 again.

7. Press Enter until you get down to *Indent*.

8. Type **20** and press Enter.

9. Draw the chart.

10. Save the chart with the name **TRAINING**.

Working with Column Charts

Harvard Graphics provides chart types for two- and three-column charts. The columns can contain text or numbers. If you enter numbers, they will automatically align on the right or at the decimal point.

*Column
headings*

Figure 5.3 shows the data form for a three-column chart. Notice that there is a special area for column headings. The headings in the printed chart will be underlined and have a slightly larger text size than the text in the rest of the table. You may want to use the Attributes key, F5, to further enhance the column headings.

```
┌─────────────────────────────────────────────────────────┐
│ ▓▓▓▓▓▓▓▓▓▓▓▓▓▓▓▓ Three Columns ▓▓▓▓▓▓▓▓▓▓▓▓▓▓▓▓▓▓▓▓▓▓▓▓ │
│                                                         │
│        Title:    Tactile Toys                           │
│        Subtitle: Medical Plans                          │
│        Footnote:                                        │
│  ─────────────────────────┬─────────────────┬─────────  │
│                           │Indemnity Plan   │HMO        │
│  ─────────────────────────┼─────────────────┼─────────  │
│        Services Available │Any doctor       │HMO facility│
│                           │                 │           │
│        Premium            │$25/month        │none       │
│                           │                 │           │
│        Deductible         │$50/year         │none       │
│                           │                 │           │
│        Co-insurance       │80% / 20%        │$5/visit   │
│                           │                 │           │
│                           │                 │           │
│  ─────────────────────────┴─────────────────┴─────────  │
│ F1-Help      F3-Save       F5-Attributes  F7-Size/Place │
│ F2-Draw chart F4-Draw/Annot                F10-Continue │
└─────────────────────────────────────────────────────────┘
```

Figure 5.3: A three-column chart

Use the Tab key to move the cursor from column to column.
When you press Tab in the last column, the cursor moves to the
first column on the next line. The Enter key moves the cursor to
the next line in the same column. So use the Tab key, not the Enter
key, when you are finished entering data for a line.

Entering chart data

Create a three-column chart that compares two medical plans. Refer to Figure 5.3 and follow these steps:

1. Create a three-column chart. (Do not keep the current data.)

2. Enter the title, subtitle, and the two column headings, as
    illustrated.

Three-column chart

3. Type the table. Use the Tab key to move from column to
    column. Leave two blank lines between each row. If you
    forget to leave the blank lines, don't worry—you will soon
    learn how to edit a chart.

4. Draw the chart. Notice that "HMO facility" is truncated.
    You can solve this problem by changing the text size and/or
    column spacing.

Column
Spacing

The F7 key lets you specify the size and placement of the chart's titles, column headings, and columnar text. Column width is controlled with the *Column Spacing* option. The default spacing is M (medium). To get less space between columns choose S (small); to get more space, choose L (large) or X (extra large).

Change the size and placement of the three column headings and the text.

1. Press the Size/Place key, F7.
2. Press Enter until you reach the column headings size (currently 5.5).
3. Type **5.0** and press Enter.
4. Change the size of the columnar text to **4.0**.
5. Move down to *Column Spacing*.
6. Press the spacebar until the *L* is highlighted.
7. Press F2 to draw the chart.
8. Save the chart with the name **MEDICAL**.

Creating a Free-Form Chart

Use the free-form chart type when none of the other types is appropriate. This chart type is similar to the simple list. You can create bullets anywhere and use any line spacing desired.

The main difference between the simple list and the free-form chart is in text placement. The simple list lets you use F7 to align the list on the left, center, or right, or to set an indent. These options are not available in a free-form chart, however; instead you must align text with the spacebar. Avoid using a free-form chart to create a list; you would have to press the spacebar the same number of times at the beginning of each line to indent the list.

Since Harvard Graphics offers only two- and three-column charts, you must use a free-form chart if your table has more than three columns. Also, remember that a two-column chart is limited to 23 lines, and a three-column chart to 14 lines. Because a free-form chart can have up to 48 lines, you may want to choose this chart type for any columnar chart with long columns.

The main liability of the free-form chart is that you cannot use Tab to go from one column to the next. You must use the spacebar to align your columns. However, unlike the two list charts, the spacing you see in the free-form chart's data form is the spacing you actually get on the drawn and printed chart. If you tried to align text with the spacebar on a simple or bullet list, the text would look aligned in the data form but not in the drawn or printed chart.

Aligning free-form text

Editing a Chart

Table 5.1 lists the keys you can use when editing a chart. Notice that there are no keys for moving text. In order to move text, you have to delete the line (Ctrl-Del), insert a line in the new location (Ctrl-Ins), and retype the text.

Key	*Description*
Ctrl-→	Go to next word
Ctrl-←	Go to previous word
Ctrl-↓	Scroll screen up one line
Ctrl-↑	Scroll screen down one line
Home	Go to first line on the screen
End	Go to last line on the screen
Ins	Insert/overtype characters
Del	Delete characters

Table 5.1: Editing Keys

Key	Description
Ctrl-Ins	Insert line
Ctrl-Del	Delete line

Table 5.1: Editing Keys (continued)

Inserting/
typing
over text

The Ins key is a toggle. The first time you press Ins, you are in Insert mode. Press Ins again and you are in Overtype mode. When the cursor is a flashing square, you are in Insert mode. When the cursor is a flashing line, you are in Overtype mode.

Follow these next steps to edit the TRAINING chart. (Refer to Table 5.1 for the editing keys.)

1.   Get the TRAINING chart.

2.   Delete the word "Conducting."

3.   Delete the line "Disciplinary Process."

4.   Insert an extra line above "Systems Training."

5.   Save the edited chart with the same name.

Changing Text Attributes

Step 3 already discussed how you can use F5-Attributes to control the appearance of the characters. Here are a few more tips for you.

To change a text attribute, make sure all lines you want to format are displayed *before* you press F5. You cannot scroll the screen once the Attributes menu is displayed.

To change the color of text, Tab to the *Color* option on the Attributes menu and press F6. You can then select a color from a list.

Step 6

Printing

15

This step explains how to produce your charts on printers and plotters. It also discusses how to print multiple charts on a page.

Options to Consider

Before printing, you should display your current chart settings to make sure they are appropriate for the chart you wish to print. As discussed previously, when you press F8 at the Main Menu, a screen displays the current settings for Orientation, Borders and Font.

On the bulleted list you created in Step 5, let's practice changing the chart options.

1. Get the OVERVIEW chart.

2. Press Esc until the Main Menu is displayed.

3. Press F8 to display the current chart options.

4. To move to the *Border* option, press Enter.

5. Press the spacebar until *Double* is selected, and then press Enter.

Adding a border

Harvard Graphics has built-in margins of one inch around the edge of the page. If you choose the *No margin* border option, Harvard will ignore these margins, allowing you to print a larger chart.

6. Press the spacebar until the *Sans serif* font is selected.

7. Press F10 to confirm your selections.

8. Press F2 to view the chart.

9. Save the chart with your new specifications.

Selecting a font

Previewing a Chart

Because printing can be a time-consuming process, you want to make sure your chart is correct before issuing the print command. When you draw a chart with the F2 key, Harvard Graphics gives a good representation of the final output. It does not, however, show you where the chart appears on the printed page; nor does it display the borders. The Preview command, available only at the Produce Output menu, gives you a better picture of your final output.

Follow these steps to preview your chart before printing:

1. From the Main Menu, choose option **6**, *Produce output.* Notice the F2-Preview command at the bottom of the screen.

2. Press F2 to preview. Your screen should look like Figure 6.1. The outer box represents a piece of paper, and the inner box is the double border you specified earlier.

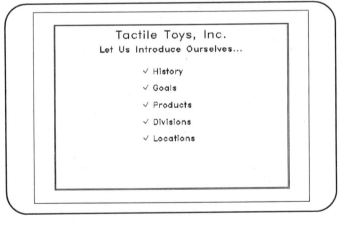

Figure 6.1: A preview of the OVERVIEW chart

Printing

To print the current chart, you choose *Printer* on the Produce Output menu. You can then adjust several print options. If you are satisfied with the default settings, just press F10 to begin printing.

From the Main Menu, or the chart data form, you can go directly to the Print Chart Options screen by using the speed key, Ctrl-P.

Print Options

Many of the settings are self-explanatory, but let's go over some of the less obvious ones. The *Quality* setting controls the print resolution—the number of dots per inch. The *High* quality option provides the best output, but takes the longest time to print. Consequently, you will probably want to choose *Draft* or *Standard* quality for your initial printout of the chart. Once you are sure the chart is perfect, change to high quality.

Print quality

Because draft quality is rough around the edges and somewhat hard to read, you may want to use high quality with a small chart. The smaller the chart size, the less print time required. The default size is *Full,* but you can choose *1/2, 1/3,* or *1/4.* Note that smaller chart sizes are not centered on the page and are always printed in landscape.

Chart sizes

Three paper sizes are available: *Letter* (8.5″ by 11″), *Wide* (14″ by 11″), and *A4* (8.25″ by 11.7″). If you have a wide-carriage printer, choose *Wide;* a full-size chart will fill the entire page.

Paper sizes

Transparencies

There are two ways to create transparencies for an overhead projector. One option is to print the chart on regular paper and photocopy it onto a transparency. Or you can print directly on the transparency.

Color printers

If you have a color printer, such as the HP PaintJet, you will probably want to print directly on the transparency so that you don't have to pay to have a color photocopy made. Check your printer manual to see if it has a special mode for printing on transparencies.

Harvard Graphics offers a special print driver just for printing transparencies on an HP PaintJet. If appropriate for your setup, you can specify this driver as your second printer *(Printer 2* on the Setup menu).

Plotting

If you frequently create charts for formal presentations, consider investing in a *plotter.* With it you can create beautiful, colorful charts. Before plotting a chart, make sure you have specified your plotter on the Setup menu. Then, to plot your charts, you'll need to

- Choose option **6**, *Produce output,* from the Main Menu.

- Choose option **2**, *Plotter.*

- Change any options in the Plot Chart Options box (explained below).

- Make sure the proper colored pens are inserted into the plotter pen holders. (The color numbers specified in the chart correspond to the plotter's pen numbers.)

- Press F10 to begin plotting.

Plot quality

As with printed charts, plotted charts can have three different quality settings, and the higher the quality, the longer the output time. Draft and standard quality do not give accurate representations of the final colors, fonts, and attributes.

Paper sizes

For plotters, only two different paper sizes are supported: *Letter* (8.5″ by 11″) and *A4* (8.25″ by 11.7″).

To plot directly onto a transparency, you need to do three things. First, load the transparency into the plotter. Second, insert special transparency pens into the pen holders. Third, turn on the *Transparency* option in the Plot Chart Options box. This option slows down the plotting speed so that the ink doesn't smear.

*Transpar-
encies*

If your chart contains more colors than your plotter has pen holders, turn on the *Pause for pen* option. When Harvard pauses, you can insert a different color pen and then press Enter to continue plotting the chart.

*Changing
plotter
pens*

Printing Multiple Charts on a Page

To print more than one chart on a page, you need to create and save a *multiple chart file*. A multiple chart indicates which charts to print and where on the page they should print. If you change any of the charts involved, the multiple chart file automatically reflects these changes.

Multiple charts have different purposes. They allow you to

- Simultaneously compare related charts
- Display a text chart that explains the data in a pictorial chart
- Create a chart that includes more lines of text than a single text chart allows

Three standard layouts are available: two, three, or four charts per page. For even more versatility, you can select a custom layout to display up to six charts, in any size and position on the page.

Create and print a multiple chart that displays two charts.

1.   From the Main Menu, choose option **1**, *Create new chart*.

2.   Choose option **7**, *Multiple chart*.

In the Multiple Chart Styles screen, the dots below each chart number indicate how the charts will be positioned in landscape orientation. In portrait, the charts are arranged differently.

3.   Choose option **2**, *Two*.

Selecting
file names

The top half of the Edit Multiple Chart screen lists the file names in the current subdirectory. If necessary, press F3 to change to a different subdirectory. To select a chart, you highlight the name and press Enter; the chart name will then appear in the *Chart* column at the bottom of the screen.

4.   Highlight WELCOME.CHT, the chart you created in Step 3, and press Enter. Notice that the chart name appears next to the number 1 in the list at the bottom of the screen.

5.   Highlight TRAINING.CHT and press Enter. This chart name appears next to 2.

6.   Press F2 to view the multiple chart. The two charts are side by side in landscape orientation, or stacked in portrait.

7.   Save the chart with the name **2CHARTS**.

8.   Print the chart.

Step 7

Pie Charts

A pie chart is one of the most commonly used business charts. By looking at the relative size of the pie slices and their accompanying percentage figures, you can clearly see the relationship between several items. Because a pie chart has only one series of data and not many options, this chart type is quick and easy to create.

In Step 7 you will build a three-dimensional pie chart that illustrates Tactile Toys' 1990 sales by product line. Only the three major product lines are included (Stuffed Animals, Dolls, and Sports); the other products are lumped into a category called Other. This chart is shown in Figure 7.1.

Although a pie can have up to 12 slices, a chart with many small slices is difficult to read. For a more attractive chart, consider combining some of the slices into a single slice labeled "Other."

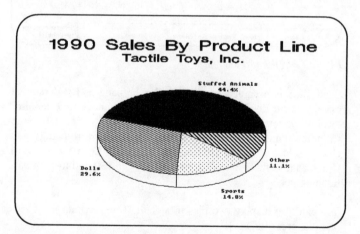

Figure 7.1: Three-dimensional pie chart

Entering Pie Chart Data

Figure 7.2 illustrates the pie chart data form. You enter the descriptive text for each slice in the *Label* column, and the numeric data in the *Value* column. The *Cut Slice* column lets you draw attention to a particular slice by separating it from the rest of the pie. (*Cut Slice* has no effect if the pie is three-dimensional.)

```
                    Pie Chart 1 Data   Page 1 of 2
Title:      1990 Sales By Product Line
Subtitle: Tactile Toys, Inc.
Footnote:

Slice         Label           Value      Cut Slice   Color   Pattern
              Name            Series 1    Yes  No

   1     Stuffed Animals      3.6            No         2       1
   2     Dolls                2.4            No         3       2
   3     Sports               1.2            No         4       3
   4     Other                0.9            No         5       4
   5                                         No         6       5
   6                                         No         7       6
   7                                         No         8       7
   8                                         No         9       8
   9                                         No        10       9
  10                                         No        11      10
  11                                         No        12      11
  12                                         No        13      12

F1-Help         F3-Save                              F9-More series
F2-Draw chart   F4-Draw/Annot   F6-Colors   F8-Options   F10-Continue
```

Figure 7.2: Pie chart data form

Each slice is assigned a unique color or pattern. By default, a color monitor displays colored slices and a monochrome monitor displays patterned slices. To change the color of a slice, tab to the *Color* column, press F6, and select a color. Unfortunately, you cannot select a pattern from a list. Appendix D in the Harvard Graphics manual displays the patterns that correspond to each pattern number.

Two pies

You can also display two pies in a chart. To enter data for a second pie, press PgDn.

Enter the data for your pie chart.

1. Create a Pie chart.

2. Enter the titles, labels, and values shown in Figure 7.2. (The values are in millions of dollars.) Remember, use Enter to move the cursor to the next line in the same column, and use Tab to move the cursor to the next column.

3. Press F2 to draw the chart.

Notice that each slice is automatically filled with a different color or pattern, and is labeled with the text and values you entered on the chart data form.

4. If you like, try different color or pattern numbers.

5. Press F3 and save the chart with the name **90PROD**.

Pie Chart Options

As with all pictorial charts, F8 displays the chart's options. Press F8 now to see what options you have. "Page 1 of 2" at the top of the options screen tells you the pie chart has two pages of options; press PgDn and PgUp to display other pages. The first page contains general pie chart options, and the second page lists options that you can change independently for Pie 1 and Pie 2.

General Pie Options

Notice that the first option page displays your titles again. Although this seems redundant, the purpose of having the titles on the options page is to let you change their Attributes (F5) and Size/Place (F7) settings. F5 and F7 work just as they did in the text charts.

Turn on the *3D effect* option.

3D effect

1. The first options page should be displayed. If necessary, press F8 to display your options, or press PgUp to display options page 1.

2. Press Enter until the cursor is next to the *3D effect* option.

3. Press the spacebar to move the pointer next to Yes.

4. Press F2 to draw the chart.

Options for two pies

Link pies and *Proportional pies* are options that apply only if you have two pies in your chart. Turn on *Link pies* if the second pie is a detailed breakdown of a single slice in the first pie. Harvard Graphics then draws lines from this slice to the second pie so that you can clearly see the relationship. Turn on the *Cut Slice* option for the slice that links the two pies.

When you turn on the *Proportional pies* option, the program totals the values in each pie and draws pies that are sized proportionally. For example, if the sum of the slices in Pie 1 is 200, and 400 for Pie 2, then Pie 2 will appear twice the size of Pie 1.

Color monitors

If you have a color monitor, you may want to change the *Fill style* option. To see both colors and patterns, you can choose *Both*. (The *Both* selection can look somewhat "busy," however.) If you don't have a color printer, try selecting *Patterns* instead of *Color* to see what the printed chart will look like.

To get gray shades instead of patterns, set the *Fill style* option to *Color* and choose Yes for the *Color* option when you print.

Individual Pie Options

The second page of options lets you change the features of each pie. Press PgDn, and let's take a look at the first group of options.

If your chart contains a single pie, press Enter to move the cursor from one option to the next in the Pie 1 column. When you press Tab, the cursor jumps back and forth between the Pie 1 and Pie 2 columns.

Chart style

Rather than arranging the data as slices in a pie, you can stack the data as blocks in a vertical column. Figure 7.3 displays a pie chart with a column style. Though not as common as round pie charts, *stacked column charts* offer yet another way of comparing data. If

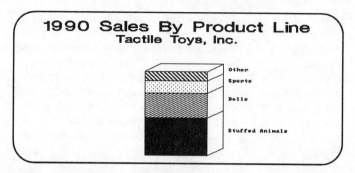

1990 Sales By Product Line
Tactile Toys, Inc.

Other
Sports
Dolls
Stuffed Animals

Figure 7.3: A column-style pie chart

your presentation contains many pie charts, you might want to avoid monotony by using the column style for a few of them.

If you didn't enter the chart data values from largest to smallest value in your chart data form, you can turn on the *Sort slices* option.   *Sort slices*

Another way to rearrange the position of the slices is with the *Starting angle* option. Enter a number between 0 and 360 degrees to rotate the slices counterclockwise. Use this option if the labels in two pie charts overlap, or if a label on one edge of the page is truncated.   *Starting angle*

To define the size of the chart, enter a number between 0 and 100 percent. The default size of both Pie 1 and Pie 2 is 50. If you don't have a Pie 2, you may want to increase the size of Pie 1.   *Pie size*

Increase the size of your pie.

1.   If necessary, press PgDn to display the second page of options.

2.   Press Enter until the cursor is next to *Pie size.*

3.   Type **75**.

4.   Press F2 to draw the chart.

Label and value options

The remaining pie chart options affect the labels, values, and percentages. Unless you indicate otherwise, Harvard Graphics displays all labels and values, and places the value below the label; percentages are not shown. If you want, you can change the size of the label (0 to 20), place the value adjacent to the label or inside the pie slice, or choose not to display the value at all. You will probably also want to format the values you display. To display values with commas and two decimal places, for example, type, **2** next to *Value format.* To display dollar signs, choose Yes for *Currency.*

Percentages

By turning on the *Show percent* option, you can display the percentage-of-the-whole value for each slice. (Harvard Graphics calculates the percentages for you.) As with other values, the percentages can be placed below or adjacent to the label or inside the slice. The default is that no decimal places are displayed in the percentage. When you need to show decimal places, type a number next to *Percent format.*

Turn off the values and turn on the percentages.

1. Press Enter until the cursor is next to *Show value,* and press the spacebar to select No.

2. Move the cursor next to *Show percent,* and press the spacebar to choose Yes.

3. Move the cursor next to *Percent format,* and type **1** to display one decimal place.

4. Draw the chart. Your chart should look similar to Figure 7.1.

5. Press Esc until the Main Menu appears.

6. Press Ctrl-S and save the chart with the same name (90PROD).

Step 8

Line Charts

Because line and bar charts are so similar, these two chart types are offered together under the *Bar/Line* chart option on the Create New Chart menu. Once you have created your chart, you then indicate which type it is. In Step 8, you will explore the options specific to line charts, as well as settings that apply to both bar and line charts. You will learn the options specific to bar charts in Step 9.

In this Step you will create a line chart that illustrates Tactile Toys' domestic (U.S.) and international sales for the period 1985 through 1990. This chart (Figure 8.1) provides two important pieces of information to new employees: the company's steady growth in the past six years, and a comparison of sales in the U.S. and international markets. The two lines on the chart, indicating domestic and international sales, are called *series*.

Figure 8.1: A line chart with two series

Choosing an X Data Type

When you create a line or bar chart, the first thing you do is define the type of data on your *x-axis*. The x-axis contains short labels that describe each data point in a series. Usually the labels are units of time (for example, months, quarters, or years). After you indicate the *X data type,* you specify the starting and ending dates or values, and the increment. Harvard Graphics then automatically creates the labels for your x-axis.

Entering labels manually

If your x-axis data are descriptive words, rather than numbers or dates, choose the *Name* option. You can then enter the x-axis labels yourself.

Create a line chart with Years as the X data type.

1. Create a *Bar/Line* chart. The X Data Type Menu appears.

2. Press the spacebar until *Year* is highlighted, and press Enter.

3. With the cursor next to *Starting with,* type **1985** and press Enter.

4. With the cursor next to *Ending with,* type **1990** and press Enter.

If the increment is 1, you can leave the *Increment* option blank.

5. Press F10 to continue.

The chart data form is displayed, and the *X Axis* column already contains the year number labels.

6. Enter the titles and values shown in Figure 8.2. (The values are in millions of dollars.) The *Series 1* column contains U.S. sales, and the *Series 2* column contains international sales.

Multiple series

Each bar/line chart can have up to eight series, with up to 240 data points per series. The first chart data form shows four series; press F9 to enter additional series.

7. Press F2 to draw the chart.

The first thing you will probably notice is that this is not a line chart. Since you haven't yet indicated the specific type of chart

```
┌─────────────────────────────────────────────────────────────────────┐
│                        Bar/Line Chart Data                   ◄    ╲  │
│                                                                       │
│      Title: U.S. and International Sales                               │
│   Subtitle: Tactile Toys, Inc.                                        │
│   Footnote:                                                           │
│                                                                       │
│            X Axis      │ Series 1 │ Series 2 │ Series 3 │ Series 4    │
│     Pt│    Year        │          │          │          │            │
│     1  │ 1985          │   0.5    │   0.1    │          │            │
│     2  │ 1986          │   0.9    │   0.2    │          │            │
│     3  │ 1987          │   1.7    │   0.7    │          │            │
│     4  │ 1988          │   3.2    │   1.1    │          │            │
│     5  │ 1989          │   5.6    │   1.9    │          │            │
│     6  │ 1990          │   8.1    │   2.3    │          │            │
│     7  │               │          │          │          │            │
│     8  │               │          │          │          │            │
│     9  │               │          │          │          │            │
│    10  │               │          │          │          │            │
│    11  │               │          │          │          │            │
│    12  │               │          │          │          │            │
│                                                                       │
│  F1-Help        F3-Save        F5-Set X type              F9-More series │
│  F2-Draw chart  F4-Draw/Annot  F6-Calculate   F8-Options  F10-Continue │
└─────────────────────────────────────────────────────────────────────┘
```

Figure 8.2: The line chart data form

you want, the default type, Bar, is used. You will change the type
in a minute. First, save the chart.

8. Press F3 to save, and enter the name **US-INTNL**.

Options

Harvard Graphics offers an abundance of options for bar/line
charts—four pages of them, to be exact.

Changing the Chart Type

Since you want this to be a line chart, you first need to change the
supplied default chart type. This is easily done by following these
steps:

1. Press F8 to display the first options page.

2. Move the cursor to the word *Bar* in the *Type* column in the
    Series 1 row.

3. Press the spacebar to highlight *Line,* instead.

4. Do the same thing for *Series 2*.

5. Draw the chart. Now, *that's* a line chart.

Other Titles

In addition to the standard titles on the chart data screen (Title, Subtitle, and Footnote), the Bar/Line chart types let you title (label) your axes. In the chart you are currently creating, it is quite clear what the x-axis labels are (years), but it is not so apparent that the y-axis is in millions of dollars. Let's label this axis.

Axis titles

Enter a title for the y-axis.

1. Move the cursor up to *Y1 axis title*.

2. Type **(In Millions)**.

3. Draw the chart.

Legends

A vital piece of information is missing from this chart: a meaningful *legend* to identify each data series. Right now the legend indicates that the line containing dots is Series 1 and the line containing crosses is Series 2. Without a more descriptive legend, you don't know what the two series represent. To enter your own legends, you simply type over the default labels in the *Legend* column of the first options page.

Enter your own legends for the line chart.

1. Move the cursor to the label "Series 1" in the *Legend* column.

2. Type **United States** and press Enter.

3. The cursor should be on the label "Series 2." Type **International**.

4. Draw the chart.

Positioning the Legend

The default position for legend is below the chart. If you like, you can move the legend almost anywhere: to the top or bottom; justified on the left, right, or center; inside or outside the chart frame. If you place the legend inside the chart, use the *Legend location* and *Legend justify* options to position the legend so that it doesn't overlap the lines or bars of the chart. You can even emphasize the legend by drawing a box around it.

In your US-INTNL chart, there is ample space for the legend inside the chart frame. In fact, by bringing the legend inside the chart frame, you will eliminate some needless white space.

1. Press PgDn to display the page 2 options.

2. Move the cursor to *Legend location*.

3. Press the spacebar to choose *Top*.

4. Move the cursor to *Legend placement, and* choose *In*.

5. Move the cursor to *Legend frame, and* choose *Single*.

6. Draw the chart. Your chart should now resemble Figure 8.1.

Moving the legend inside Framing a legend

Grid Lines

As you may have noticed, Harvard Graphics draws horizontal dotted lines from each *tick mark* on the y-axis. These *grid lines* help you identify the values associated with each data point. The third option page contains settings for grid lines on both axes. You also have options for drawing dotted lines, solid lines, or no lines from the tick marks on each axis. In most bar and line charts, you will use either horizontal grid lines (like the default) or no grid lines at all.

Harvard Graphics offers more precise ways of identifying data values in bar and line charts. If you select *All* for the *Value labels* option (options page 2), each data point is labeled with its associated value. The *Data Table* option (options page 3) creates a minispreadsheet of your values at the bottom of the chart.

Identifying Each Series

There are three ways to identify your data series in line charts: with colors, markers, and line styles. These selections are on options page 4.

Colors

To change the color of a series, tab to the *Color* column of the series you want to change, and press F6. You can then choose a color from the list.

Markers

You can select from thirteen different symbols for the identifying markers in a line chart. These symbols are illustrated in Appendix D of the Harvard Graphics manual. To try a different marker, tab to the *Marker/Pattern* column of the series you want to change, and type the new number.

Line styles

Harvard Graphics uses a thin, solid line for each series unless you specify otherwise. Table 8.1 lists the other available line styles.

Number	Style
1	Thin, solid line
2	Thick, solid line
3	Dotted line
4	Dashed line

Table 8.1: Line Styles

Choosing a different line style for each series helps differentiate the series lines. For example, in a chart that illustrates actual versus projected sales, you can use a solid line for actual sales and a dotted line for projected sales.

Too Many Options?

The number of options Harvard Graphics offers is both a blessing and a curse. It's wonderful to have options to customize your chart in every imaginable way. However, you may find it difficult to keep all the options straight and to remember on which page the option is located. Here are a few tips for you.

- If you can't find an option on the current page, press PgDn to go to the next page. When you get to the last option page, PgDn circles you back to the first page.

- If you can't remember which option you need, press F1 and read the Help screens. Some Help screens have multiple pages; press PgDn to read additional screens.

- If you really get stumped about what options to use, create a chart from the Gallery, as explained in Step 3. That way your options will be set automatically.

Before you go on to the next Step, save your chart with the same name.

Step 9

Bar Charts

Because the same menu option is used to create both bar and line charts, you can apply most of what you learned in Step 8 to creating bar charts. Some of the material here in Step 9 will be a review, but you will also learn many new charting features.

Figure 9.1 displays the bar chart you will design in Step 9. This chart informs new employees about the sales of the major product lines in each regional division. For example, from this chart a new employee can see that the North-West region sells the fewest toys, and that the South-West division sells the most sports items. Notice that the four data series (the portions of the bar representing each product) are stacked on top of each other. This *stacked bar* is one of several styles available for bar charts. Also, the chart is enhanced with a three-dimensional effect.

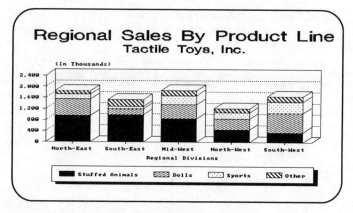

Figure 9.1: A three-dimensional stacked bar chart

Entering Data

As with line charts, the first step to creating a bar chart is to choose an X data type (for example, Days, Months, or Quarters). The line chart you created in Step 8 had Years along the x-axis.

You can see that Figure 9.1 does not use one of the X data types that automatically fill in the dates or numbers. This x-axis contains labels (North-East, South-East, and so on). You must therefore select the *Name* X data type, and then enter the labels yourself. Let's do this.

Enter the data for the bar chart.

1. Create a Bar/Line chart. The X Data Type Menu is displayed.

2. Since *Name* is already highlighted, press F10 to continue.

3. Enter chart titles, x-axis names, and series values as shown in Figure 9.2. (The values are in thousands of dollars.) The *Series1* column contains data for the stuffed animal product line, *Series 2* contains doll data, *Series 3* contains sports data, and *Series 4* contains data for all other product lines.

4. Draw the chart.

Cluster-style bars

Notice that the bars are placed side by side, instead of stacked on top of each other as they are in Figure 9.1. This is because the

```
┌──────────────────────────────────────────────────────────────────────┐
│                        Bar/Line Chart Data                             │
│  ═══════════════════════════════════════════════════════════════════  │
│      Title: Regional Sales By Product Line                             │
│   Subtitle: Tactile Toys, Inc.                                         │
│   Footnote:                                                            │
│                                                                        │
│                X Axis      Series 1   Series 2   Series 3   Series 4   │
│       Pt       Name                                                    │
│                                                                        │
│        1   North-East        950        600        170        130      │
│        2   South-East        990        200        100        240      │
│        3   Mid-West          850        500        330        180      │
│        4   North-West        450        400        220        150      │
│        5   South-West        360        700        400        200      │
│        6                                                               │
│        7                                                               │
│        8                                                               │
│        9                                                               │
│       10                                                               │
│       11                                                               │
│       12                                                               │
│                                                                        │
│   F1-Help         F3-Save       F5-Set X type            F9-More series │
│   F2-Draw chart   F4-Draw/Annot F6-Calculate  F8-Options  F10-Continue  │
└──────────────────────────────────────────────────────────────────────┘
```

Figure 9.2: The bar chart data form

chart uses the default bar style, which is *Cluster* not *Stack*. Later in this step you will experiment with different bar styles.

5. Press F3 and name the chart **REGIONS**.

Bar Chart Options

In Step 8, I skipped over some of the chart options because they weren't applicable to line charts, or they didn't apply to the particular chart you were creating. In this Step, however, you will get an opportunity to explore more of the options.

Titles and Legends

Your chart so far lacks the axis titles and descriptive legends shown in Figure 9.1. Remember, the first options page has space for this information. Let's enter the titles for the x- and y-axes, and the product line descriptions as a legend. Follow these steps:

1. Press F8 to display the first options page.

2. Enter the *X axis* and *Y1 axis* titles shown in the screen in Figure 9.3.

3. Enter the product names (**Stuffed Animals, Dolls, Sports,** and **Other**) shown in the *Legend Title* column of Figure 9.3.

Axis titles

Note: If you are typing a new legend that is shorter than the existing legend text, be sure to delete the remaining existing text. You can use either Del or the spacebar.

4. Draw the chart.

Unlike the line chart you created earlier, the inside of the chart frame does not contain much extra space; therefore, you should keep the legend where it currently is—at the bottom of the chart. To separate the legend text from the labels under the chart bars, you can place a box around the legend. The *Legend frame* setting is on options page 2.

Framing the legend

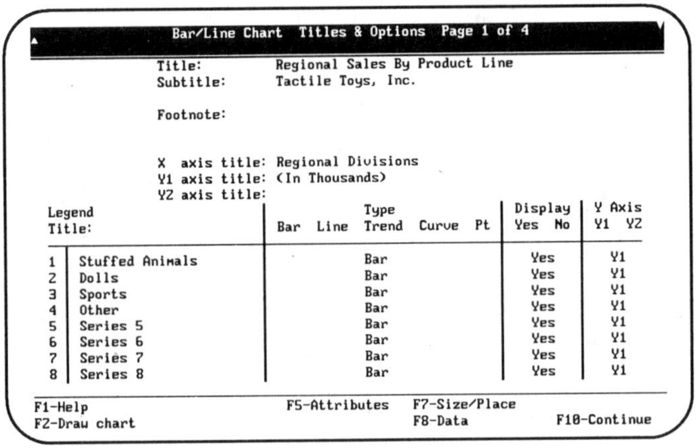

```
┌─────────────────────────────────────────────────────────────┐
│        Bar/Line Chart  Titles & Options  Page 1 of 4          │
│                                                               │
│        Title:        Regional Sales By Product Line           │
│        Subtitle:     Tactile Toys, Inc.                       │
│                                                               │
│        Footnote:                                              │
│                                                               │
│        X  axis title: Regional Divisions                      │
│        Y1 axis title: (In Thousands)                          │
│        Y2 axis title:                                         │
│  Legend                        Type          Display │ Y Axis │
│  Title:              Bar  Line Trend Curve Pt Yes No │ Y1  Y2 │
│                                                               │
│   1 │ Stuffed Animals         Bar            Yes      Y1      │
│   2 │ Dolls                   Bar            Yes      Y1      │
│   3 │ Sports                  Bar            Yes      Y1      │
│   4 │ Other                   Bar            Yes      Y1      │
│   5 │ Series 5                Bar            Yes      Y1      │
│   6 │ Series 6                Bar            Yes      Y1      │
│   7 │ Series 7                Bar            Yes      Y1      │
│   8 │ Series 8                Bar            Yes      Y1      │
│                                                               │
│  F1-Help               F5-Attributes   F7-Size/Place          │
│  F2-Draw chart                         F8-Data     F10-Continue│
└─────────────────────────────────────────────────────────────┘
```

Figure 9.3: Titles and legends for REGIONS chart

Follow these steps to create a shadowed box around the legend.

1. Press PgDn to display the second options page.

2. Move the cursor next to *Legend frame.*

3. Press the spacebar until the pointer is next to *Shadow.*

4. Draw the chart.

Bar Styles

You have already seen two of the bar chart styles Harvard Graphics offers: Cluster (your current chart) and Stack (Figure 9.1). Table 9.1 gives a summary of the available bar styles.

Bar Chart Style	*Description*
Cluster	Bars are placed side by side.
Overlap	In each cluster of bars, part of one bar slightly overlaps an adjacent bar.

Table 9.1: Bar Styles

Bar Chart Style	Description
Stack	Bars are stacked on top of one another.
100%	The y-axis is scaled from 0 to 100%, and the series are stacked. This chart, like a pie chart, shows the proportion each series contributes to the whole.
Step	Bars are stacked, with no space in between.
Paired	A horizontal bar chart, with the vertical axis in the middle instead of on the left. One set of bars extends to the left of the vertical axis, and the other extends to the right.

Table 9.1: Bar Styles (continued)

The best way to understand these styles is to try out each one. *Bar style* is a setting on options page 2, the screen you probably now have displayed. One by one, select each style and draw the chart. After you have seen each style, select *Stack*.

An additional chart style is located further down on this second options page: *Horizontal chart*. This style reverses the x- and y-axes.

Horizontal charts

Bar Enhancements

To make your bar charts look more professional, you can add special effects. Table 9.2 lists the available enhancements. Not all effects work with all bar styles. Unless you specify otherwise, bars have no enhancements (the *None* setting is the default).

Enhancement	Description
3D	Three-dimensional (not available with the Paired style).
Shadow	A dark shadow appears behind the bars (with Cluster, Stack, and 100% bar styles only).

Table 9.2: Bar Enhancements

Enhancement	Description
Link	Dotted lines connect each series in stacked bars (with Stack and 100% bar styles only).

Table 9.2: Bar Enhancements (continued)

Because your current chart style is a stacked bar, you can try out all of the enhancements. One by one, select each enhancement and draw the chart. After you have viewed each enhancement, select the 3D effect.

Other Bar Options

Options page 2 lists several other options specific to bar charts.

- *Bar fill style*
- *Bar width*
- *Bar overlap*
- *Bar depth*

Let's go over each one briefly.

Bar fill style

If you have a color monitor, you may want to change the *Bar fill style* option. To see both colors and patterns, you can choose *Both.* If you don't have a color printer, you may want to select *Patterns* instead of *Color,* so that you can see what the printed chart will look like. If you choose the *Color* fill style, and turn on the *Color* print option, the bars print with different grey shades.

To change the color or pattern assigned to each series, go to options page 4.

Bar width

The *Bar width* option lets you create wider or narrower bars, by entering a number between 1 and 100. The larger the value, the wider the bar. If you leave this option blank, Harvard Graphics calculates the width for you.

The *Bar overlap* option indicates the percentage of overlap between bars in the Overlap style. You enter a number of degrees between 1 and 100. The default is 50, meaning that half of one bar overlaps the adjacent bar.

The *Bar depth* option allows you to control the depth of three-dimensional bars. Enter a number between 1 and 100. The larger the number, the deeper the bar. The default is 25.

Formatting the Y-Axis

If you had to draw a chart by hand, one of your initial tasks would be to determine a scale for your y-axis. You would need to decide what sort of increments to use for each tick mark, and with what values to begin and end the scale. To save you time, Harvard Graphics automatically determines an appropriate scale for the y-axis, based on the values in the chart data form. In some charts, though, you may want to override the automatic scaling and enter your own values. You can format the y-axis on the third options page.

Even though the scale on your stacked bar chart works fine, let's practice changing the scale.

1. Press PgDn to go to the third options page.

2. In the table at the bottom of the screen, move the cursor to the *Y1 Axis* column, in the *Format* row.

3. Type a comma to display commas in the numbers.

4. Move the cursor to the *Maximum Value* row, and type **2400**.

5. Move the cursor to the *Increment* row, and type **400**.

6. Draw the chart.

7. Go to the Main Menu and save the chart with the same name (REGIONS).

Step 10

Area Charts

An *area chart* is a cross between a line and a bar chart. Like a line chart, lines in the area chart connect each data point. Like a bar chart, patterns or colors are used to represent each series. Figure 10.1 shows an example of an area chart.

Because of the similarities between these chart types, creating an area chart is not too different from creating line and bar charts. In fact, you can easily take the data from a bar/line chart and turn it into an area chart. And that is exactly what you are going to do in this Step.

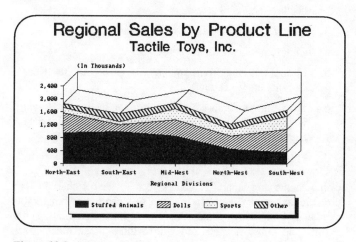

Figure 10.1: An area chart

Creating an Area Chart

If you were creating an area chart from scratch, you would choose option 1, *Create new chart*, followed by option 4, *Area*. You would then specify the type of data for the chart's x-axis (for example, *Name, Month,* or *Quarter*) and then complete the chart data form. If you need to review this process, go back to Step 8.

*Using
another
chart's
data*

For the area chart in this Step, you will use the data from the bar chart you created in Step 9. Using data from an existing chart is a two-step process. First, you retrieve the chart. Second, you create a new chart. This time, when you see the "Keep current data" question, you answer Yes to tell Harvard you want to use the data from the current (retrieved) chart.

In this exercise, you will create an area chart of Tactile Toys' regional sales by product line. The data from this chart already exists in the REGIONS bar chart.

1. Press Ctrl-G to get a chart.

2. Highlight REGIONS.CHT and press Enter. The three-dimensional stacked bar chart you created in the last step is displayed on your screen.

3. Press Esc until the Main Menu appears.

4. Choose option **1**, *Create new chart.*

5. Choose option **4**, *Area.* You are prompted with the "Keep current data" question.

6. Press Enter to choose Yes. Because you instructed Harvard Graphics to keep the existing data, the regional sales data automatically displays in the area chart data form.

7. Press F2 to draw the area chart.

Compare the area chart on your screen to the bar chart in Figure 9.1, and you will notice that the two charts are remarkably similar. In both charts, the product lines (Stuffed Animals, Dolls, Sports, and Other) are stacked with a three-dimensional effect, and each series is represented by a different pattern or color. The area chart, however, displays a solid area of varying heights to represent the different series, rather than separate bars.

By answering Yes to the "Keep current data" question, you also kept the existing chart's options and titles. Notice that the y-axis scale automatically is formatted with commas, and the legend has a shadow box around it.

Options

The options for area charts are virtually identical to bar/line chart options. Four option pages are available; only the options that apply especially to area charts will be discussed here.

First Options Page

Press F8 to display the first options page. Among other things, this page lets you add, modify, and format titles. Remember, to change the size or placement of the title, press F7. To assign attributes to text, press F5.

Notice that the *Type* column contains "Area" for each series. When you create an area chart from scratch or use the data from an existing *bar* chart, the chart type is automatically set to Area. If you want a series to be a different type, you can choose from three other chart variations: Line, Trend, and Bar. When you use the data from an existing *line* chart, the chart type is set to Line, not Area.

Other chart types

To change the type designation, place the cursor in the *Type* column and press the spacebar until the type desired is selected. Repeat for each series.

Chart Styles and Enhancements

Press PgDn to view options page 2. As you can see, Harvard Graphics offers three different styles for the area chart: Stack, Overlap, and 100%.

Stack, the default area chart style, layers the series on top of one another so that you can easily see the cumulative total of the series. The first series appears as the bottom layer and the last series as the top. For the most visually appealing stacked area chart, place the series with the largest volume at the bottom of the chart.

Stack

In the Overlap chart type, each series begins at ground zero—at the bottom (usually zero) of the y-axis scale. If you don't need for

Overlap

the chart to display the series totals, use the Overlap style instead of Stack. Figure 10.2 displays an overlapped area chart. This chart uses the same data as the line chart you created in Step 8, USINTNL.CHT.

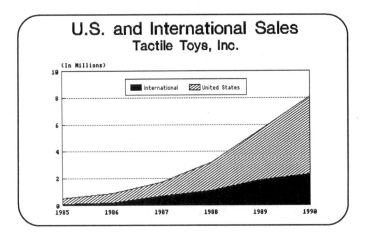

Figure 10.2: Overlap-style area chart

If the numeric values in your first series are greater than those in the other series, the pattern or color of the first series will block out all others. Thus, you will not be able to see the other series. To avoid this problem, enter the series of data from smallest to greatest volume. (This rule is the reverse of the one previously mentioned for stacked area charts.)

100%   In the 100% area chart style, the y-axis is scaled from 0 to 100%, and the series are stacked. This chart, like a pie chart, shows the proportion each series contributes to the whole. Figure 10.3 displays a 100% area chart.

3D   Only one enhancement is offered for area charts: *3D*. This effect gives depth to your chart. It is especially useful in Overlap-style charts, to let your audience readily identify that the series are not stacked. Figure 10.4 illustrates an Overlap area chart with a three-dimensional enhancement.

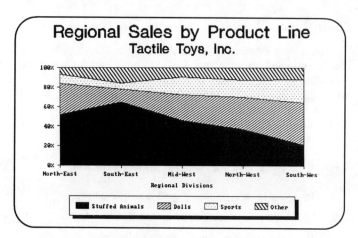

Figure 10.3: 100% area chart

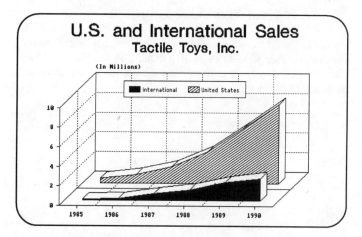

Figure 10.4: A three-dimensional Overlap-style area chart

Other Options

The remaining options are identical to those found in bar/line charts. To review these options, look at Steps 8 and 9. One option you may want to consider is grid lines. Because there is little white space in a stacked area chart, the y-axis grid lines are not as helpful as they are in other chart types. However, in a three-dimensional Overlap-style area chart, you may want to use both x- and y-axis grid lines.

Turn off the y-axis grid lines for your stacked area chart.

1. Press PgDn until options page 3 is displayed.

2. Move the cursor down to *Y1 Grid Lines.*

3. Press the spacebar until *None* is highlighted.

4. Draw the chart.

5. Save the chart with the name **REGIONS2.**

If you later want to retrieve this chart, you may not be able to remember whether REGIONS or REGIONS2 is the chart's name. You won't need to guess at it—simply look in the *Type* column on the Select Chart screen.

Step 11

High/Low/Close Charts

The primary use for the *high/low/close chart* is to graph the fluctuations in stock prices. This chart type usually has four series:
High, Low, Close, and Open. *High* is the stock's highest price of
the time period (for example, day, month, quarter, or year), *Low*
is the lowest price, *Close* is the final price at the end of the time
period, and *Open* is the initial price at the beginning of the
time period.

Figure 11.1 is an example of this chart type. The high and low
data points are connected to form a rectangular bar. The closing
price is a horizontal line that crosses the right side of the bar, and
the opening price line crosses on the left.

This chart type is not restricted to stock data. You can also graph
other types of high/low data such as temperatures, test scores,
sales, and project bids.

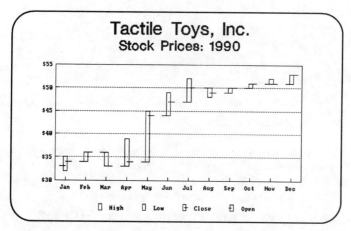

Figure 11.1: A high/low/close chart

Creating a High/Low/Close Chart

Although this chart type automatically gives you four series (High, Low, Close, and Open), you do not need to use all four; just fill in data for the ones you want. If you enter either Close or Open data, the data point is represented by a single horizontal line across both sides of the bar. If your chart has both Close and Open data, the lines appear on opposite sides of the bar: Close on the right, Open on the left.

Additional series

Actually, you are allowed up to eight series in a high/low/close chart. To enter additional series, press F9 at the chart data form. Series 5–8 can be displayed as lines or bars. You may want to use these "bonus" series for displaying averages or trends.

In this exercise, you will create a chart that illustrates the price fluctuations of Tactile Toys' stock in 1990.

1. From the Main Menu, choose option **1**, *Create new chart.*

2. Choose option **5**, *High/Low/Close.* The X Data Type Menu appears.

3. Press the spacebar until *Month* is highlighted, and press Enter.

4. With the cursor next to *Starting with,* type **Jan** and press Enter.

5. With the cursor next to *Ending with,* type **Dec.**

6. Press F10 to continue.

The chart data form is displayed, and the *X Axis* column is filled in with the months January through December.

7. Enter the titles and values shown in Figure 11.2.

8. Press F3 and save the chart with the name **STOCK90.**

9. Press F2 to draw the chart.

High/Low/Close Chart Data

Title: Tactile Toys, Inc.
Subtitle: Stock Prices: 1990
Footnote:

Pt	X Axis Month	High	Low	Close	Open
1	Jan	35	32	34	33
2	Feb	36	34	36	34
3	Mar	36	33	33	36
4	Apr	39	33	34	33
5	May	45	34	44	34
6	Jun	49	44	47	44
7	Jul	52	47	50	47
8	Aug	50	48	49	50
9	Sep	50	49	50	49
10	Oct	51	50	51	50
11	Nov	52	51	51	51
12	Dec	53	51	53	51

F1-Help   F3-Save   F5-Set X type   F9-More series
F2-Draw chart   F4-Draw/Annot   F6-Calculate   F8-Options   F10-Continue

Figure 11.2: The high/low/close data form

Make sure all the Open and Close lines touch the High/Low bar. If
the lines are above or below the rectangular bar, the data is in-
accurate; opening and closing data must be within the monthly
high-low range.

Options

Like bar/line charts, the high/low/close chart has four pages of options, and the options for the two chart types correspond closely.
The remainder of this chapter discusses the options unique to
high/low/close charts. From the chart data form, press F8 now
to display the first options page.

This chart type is the only one that automatically enters legends
for you. Notice that High, Low, Close, and Open are entered in
the *Legend* column. You can modify the text if you like. One
option you cannot change on this screen, however, is the *Type* for
series 1–4. The first series is always High, the second is
Low, and so forth.

Legends

If you have entered data for a series, but don't want it displayed in
the chart, you can hide it. It's better to turn off the display rather

*Hiding a
series*

than to delete the data—just in case you later decide you do want to display the series. Let's try turning off the Close and Open series.

1. Move the cursor to the *Display* column in the *Close* row.

2. Press the spacebar to set the display to *No*.

3. Repeat these two steps to turn off the *Open* series.

4. Draw the chart. The horizontal lines are now hidden, and the legends have disappeared for the Open and Close series.

Styles

The second options page includes several style settings. Press PgDn now to display this options page. *Bar style* affects only bars in series 5–8; it has no affect for the High, Low, Close, and Open series. *High/Low style* is the main option for this chart type. The default style, Bar, connects the High and Low data points to form a rectangular bar.

Area style

The Area style for a high/low/close chart shades the range between the High and Low values, along with the area between data points. Figure 11.3 illustrates this type of chart. Because this style does not show the data points for the Open or Close series, you should turn off the display of these two series. If you don't, the legends will still display.

Error bar

The *Error bar* style is similar to the Bar style, except that a thin vertical line instead of a rectangular bar connects the High and Low values.

Bar fill style

If your chart has additional series (5–8) that are bars, the *Bar fill* style option lets you fill these bars with colors, patterns, or both. It does *not* refer to the rectangular bars displayed in the Bar style chart.

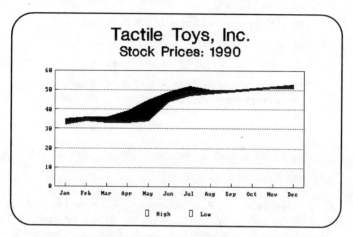

Figure 11.3: Area style on a high/low/close chart

If you want to shade the rectangles in the Bar style chart, choose *Color* for the *Bar fill style* option *and* turn on the *Color* option on the Print Chart Options menu. On a color monitor, you will see a solid color. On a monochrome monitor, the bars won't be filled in on the screen—you'll only see the shade when you print.

The *Bar width* option allows you to change the width of the rectangles in the Bar style chart. Enter a number between 1 and 100. If you leave the option blank, Harvard Graphics determines the width for you. A value of 100 makes the bars so wide that there is no space between the bars. For your chart, change the width to **35**.

Bar width

Formatting the Y-Axis

Draw your current chart, and look at the y-axis. Because stock prices are in currency, you need to add dollar signs to the numbers on the y-axis. Also, since the 1990 stock prices do not dip below 32, the scale could start at 30 instead of zero. (The data points are easier to decipher with a reduced y-axis range.) You will often find that you want to change the minimum and maximum values for the y-axis in high/low/close charts. Let's do this now.

1. Press PgDn until options page 3 is displayed.

2. Move the cursor next to *Y1 Axis Labels.*

3. Press the spacebar until *Currency* is marked.

4. Move down into the table at the bottom of the screen. Place the cursor in the *Y1 Axis* column in the *Minimum Value* row.

5. Type **30** and press Enter.

6. In the *Maximum Value* row, type **55**.

7. Draw the chart.

The numbers on the y-axis now have dollar signs, and range from 30 to 55. Because of this limited scale, the stock's substantial upward trend is more noticeable. Also, each of the bars is longer.

8. Press Esc until the Main Menu is displayed.

9. Save the chart with the same name (STOCK90).

Step 12

Organization Charts

The most common use for an organization chart is to illustrate a corporation's structure. This chart, commonly referred to as an *org chart,* identifies the names and titles of the key players in a company or division. Figure 12.1 is a simplified org chart for Tactile Toys.

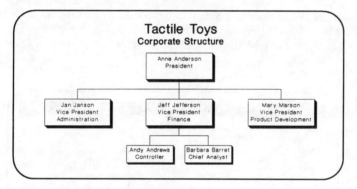

Figure 12.1: An organization chart

Here are a few other ways to use organization charts:

- A flowchart for a computer program
- An outline of tasks to be performed in a project
- A diagram of a hard disk's directory structure

Organization Chart Terminology

Before you create your first org chart, you need to understand a few terms. A *manager* is the person (or item) for which you are currently entering information; for example, the president is usually the first manager in the chart. The people (or items) at the next level down are called *subordinates*. In Figure 12.1, the subordinates of manager Anderson are Janson, Jefferson, and Marson. The subordinates of manager Jefferson are Andrews and Barret. Depending on the level, the same person can be a subordinate and a manager.

All information about each manager is entered into a separate data form. Figure 12.2 shows the data form for manager Anderson. Into this form you type the manager's full name, title, and comment, along with any subordinates' names. Optionally, you may enter 11-character-long abbreviations for the name, title, and comment. If your chart has many subordinates and becomes too crowded, Harvard Graphics offers an option to display only the abbreviations.

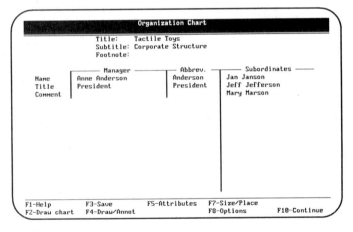

Figure 12.2: The data form for the first manager, Anderson

In this exercise, you will create an org chart that informs new employees about the corporate structure of Tactile Toys.

1. From the Main Menu, choose option **1**, *Create new chart*.

2. Choose option **6**, *Organization*.

3. As shown in Figure 12.2, enter the title, subtitle, and manager information, including subordinate names.

Remember, press Enter to move the cursor to the next line in the same column, and Tab to move the cursor to the next column.

4. Press F2 to draw the chart.

Notice that the second level—currently the last level—is displayed vertically instead of horizontally. The default is that the last level is displayed vertically. You will change this default later.

Defining Subordinates

Your next step is to enter information (title, comments, abbreviations, and subordinates) for each of the three subordinates. To display the data form for a subordinate, press Ctrl-PgDn. This takes you to the next level in the org chart. Once you are at this level, you can press PgDn to display the data form for the next subordinate, or PgUp to see the previous subordinate. The best way to understand this process is to do it.

Complete your org chart by filling in the subordinate data.

1. Place the cursor on the first subordinate name, Janson.

2. Press Ctrl-PgDn to display this subordinate's data form. It appears with the manager's name, Jan Janson, filled in.

3. Press Tab to move the cursor next to *Title*.

4. Enter **Vice President** for the title.

5. Enter **Administration** for the comment.

6. Enter appropriate abbreviations (for example, Janson, VP, Admin) to be used when necessary.

7. Press PgDn to display the next subordinate's data form. The data form for Jeff Jefferson appears.

8. Refer to Figure 12.3 to complete the data form. Be sure you enter the names in the Subordinates column.

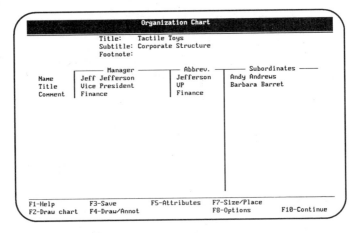

```
                    Organization Chart

              Title:     Tactile Toys
              Subtitle:  Corporate Structure
              Footnote:

                 — Manager —      — Abbrev. —     — Subordinates —
       Name    | Jeff Jefferson  | Jefferson     Andy Andrews
       Title   | Vice President  | UP            Barbara Barret
       Comment | Finance         | Finance



  F1-Help        F3-Save        F5-Attributes   F7-Size/Place
  F2-Draw chart  F4-Draw/Annot                  F8-Options      F10-Continue
```

Figure 12.3: Jefferson's data form

9. Press PgDn to enter data for the next subordinate. You'll get the data form for Mary Marson.

10. Enter **Vice President** for the title.

11. Enter **Product Development** for the comment.

12. Enter appropriate abbreviations.

13. Press F2 to draw the chart.

The second level of the chart now displays horizontally because it is no longer the last level. Also, notice that the comments you entered are not shown. The options screen lets you turn on the display of comments. Now all that's left to finish the chart is to enter the titles for Jefferson's subordinates (Andrews and Barret). To enter this information, you need to navigate back to Jefferson's data form. The PgUp key displays the previous subordinate at the same level.

1. Press PgUp to display Jefferson's form.

2. Place the cursor on Andy Andrews.

3. Press Ctrl-PgDn to display this subordinate's data form.

4. Press Tab and type **Controller** for the title.

5. Press PgDn to display the form for the next subordinate, Barret.

6. Type **Chief Analyst** for the title.

7. Draw the chart. Notice that the titles you just entered do not display. To display the titles in the last level of the chart, you can change an option (discussed in the following section).

8. Press F3 and save the chart with the name **ORGCHART.**

Options

Unlike the other chart types you have seen so far, the organization chart has only a single page of options. Press F8 now, and let's go through each of these options.

The first two options let you designate a starting point for the display of the org chart. With the *Start chart at* option, you can begin the chart display with either the first level *(Top)*—the default—or the manager currently displayed on the data form *(Current manager)*. Remember, to change the current level, press Ctrl-PgUp or Ctrl-PgDn when you are at a chart data form.

Displaying levels

The *Levels to show* option lets you control how many levels are displayed on the chart. Counting begins with the level you indicated for the *Start chart at* option. The default is that all levels are displayed.

Unless you specify otherwise, titles are shown for all levels except for the last one, and comments are not shown for any of the levels. You can find the options for the last level at the bottom of the options screen.

Showing titles and comments

If you record abbreviations for name, title, and comment in the data forms, you can display them by turning on the Abbreviations option. Abbreviations are helpful when your chart has many subordinates. Because Harvard must make the text small enough to fit

Abbreviations

all the boxes across the chart, this small type can make the org chart difficult to read. Since Harvard Graphics does not offer a way to change the type size, a solution is to display the abbreviations, which automatically will appear in a larger type.

Shadow

Shadow boxes are a nice effect to add to your org charts. Figure 12.1 shows you how shadow boxes look.

Adding style to text

Though you cannot change the size of the text inside the boxes, you can change the text style *(Light, Italic, Bold)* and color. The style of the names, titles, and comments can be changed independently of one another. The *Split* option lets you control whether the text is split among multiple lines. The default is that the first and last names are split; the titles and comments are not.

Horizontal vs. vertical

The last option on the screen, *Arrangement,* controls whether the last level of the chart is arranged horizontally or vertically. If you want the last level to display in the same way as the other levels, choose *Horizontal.*

Change some of the options for your org chart. The options page should already be on your screen. If it's not, press F8.

1. Move the cursor to *Show comments.*

2. Press the spacebar to select Yes.

3. Turn on the *Shadow* option.

4. Move the cursor to *Names.*

5. Tab to the *Split* option and select No.

6. Move the cursor to *Titles,* and choose *Light.*

7. Move the cursor down to the *Last Level* area.

8. Turn on the titles and change the arrangement to *Horizontal.*

9. Display the chart. Your chart should now resemble Figure 12.1.

10. Return to the Main Menu.

11. Save the chart with the same name.

Modifying the Chart

Harvard Graphics provides several commands for modifying your org chart. You can insert, delete, and move subordinates. These commands, along with the navigation keys you previously learned, are listed in Table 12.1.

For your own protection, Harvard Graphics does not let you delete a manager that has subordinates.

Key Combination	Description
Ctrl-Del	Deletes name
Ctrl-Ins	Inserts a name
Ctrl-↑	In a list of subordinates, moves a name up
Ctrl-↓	Moves a name down
Ctrl-PgDn/PgUp	Displays data form at next/previous level
PgDn/PgUp	Displays next/previous subordinate at the same level

Table 12.1: Editing Commands for Organization Charts

Step 13

Slide Shows

With Harvard Graphics' *slide show* feature, you won't need to create overhead transparencies or 35-mm slides for your presentations—you can display the charts right on the computer screen. Of course, for a large audience, you will want to project the images on a big screen.

A second reason to create a slide show is to print a group of charts (up to 90) without having to issue the Get and Print commands for each chart. This process is called *batch printing*. One of my clients had 75 charts to print for a presentation. She created a slide show, told Harvard Graphics to print the show, and went home for the evening. When she came back the next morning, all of her charts were printed—and she didn't have to work overtime!

Creating a Slide Show

The basic steps for making a slide show are as follows:

- First create a list of the charts you want to include in the show, in the order you want them to appear.

- Then, add special effects. You can control how the charts are drawn on and erased from the screen, and the individual display time for each chart in the show.

- As necessary, add, delete, or reorganize the charts in the show.

In this exercise, you will create a slide show file.

1. From the Main Menu, choose option **7**, *Slide show menu*.

2. Choose option **1**, *Create slide show*.

3. Enter **EMP-SHOW** for the slide show file name.

This file will contain the list of chart names in your slide show. The file is stored when you exit the Create/Edit Slide Show screen; you don't need to issue a save command. Slide show files have the extension .SHW.

4. Enter a description for the file, **New Employee Presentation**, and press F10.

Selecting Files

The Create/Edit Slide Show screen is shown in Figure 13.1. This screen has two separate areas. The top area contains a list of .CHT files in the current directory. The bottom area lists the files in your slide show; this area is called your *show list*. As you select files from the top area, the names are displayed in the show list.

```
                        Create/Edit Slide Show
  Filename Ext     Date        Type             Description
           1
  OVERVIEW.CHT    06/27/90    BULLET    Tactile Toys, Inc.
  REGIONS .CHT    06/27/90    BAR/LINE  Regional Sales by Product Line
  STOCK90 .CHT    06/27/90    H/L/C     1990 stock prices
  TRAINING.CHT    06/27/90    LIST      Tactile Toys
  US-INTNL.CHT    06/27/90    BAR/LINE  U.S. and International Sales
  WELCOME .CHT    06/27/90    TITLE     New Employee


  Show name: EMP-SHOW.SHW
  - Order ———— File ———— Type ———————— Description ——————
      1        OVERVIEW.CHT




  Show description: New Employee Presentation

  F1-Help
                                                    F10-Continue
```

Figure 13.1: The Create/Edit Slide Show screen

A slide show can only contain charts from a single directory. If your charts are scattered around your hard disk, consolidate them into one directory before you create the slide show.

To select a chart for your slide show, use the arrow keys to highlight the name in the top area, and then press Enter. Mouse users can point to the name and click. The file will then appear in your slide show list at the bottom of the screen.

Select several charts to appear in your presentation to new employees. This exercise uses charts that you built in previous Steps.
If you don't have one of the indicated charts, either leave it out or
choose a different one.

1. Use the arrow keys or mouse to highlight
   WELCOME.CHT.

2. Press Enter or click the left mouse button.

The WELCOME.CHT file is now listed next to number 1 in the
Order column. The welcoming message in this title chart will be
the first slide in the presentation.

3. For the second chart, highlight OVERVIEW.CHT and
   press Enter.

4. Continue to select the following charts in this order:
   90PROD.CHT, REGIONS.CHT, and ORGCHART.CHT.
   Compare your final show list to the one in Figure 13.2.

```
                        Create/Edit Slide Show
 ┌──────────────┬──────────┬──────────┬────────────────────────────────────┐
 │ Filename Ext │   Date   │   Type   │             Description            │
 ├──────────────┼──────────┼──────────┼────────────────────────────────────┤
 │ 90PROD  .CHT │ 06/27/90 │ PIE      │ 1990 Sales by Product Line         │
 │ ORGCHART.CHT │ 06/27/90 │ ORG      │ Tactile Toys                       │
 │ OVERVIEW.CHT │ 06/27/90 │ BULLET   │ Tactile Toys, Inc.                 │
 │ REGIONS .CHT │ 06/27/90 │ BAR/LINE │ Regional Sales by Product Line     │
 │ STOCK90 .CHT │ 06/27/90 │ H/L/C    │ 1990 stock prices                  │
 │ TRAINING.CHT │ 06/27/90 │ LIST     │ Tactile Toys                       │
 └──────────────┴──────────┴──────────┴────────────────────────────────────┘

 Show name: EMP-SHOW.SHW
 - Order ────────┬─ File ──────┬─ Type ────┬──────── Description ────────
      1          │ WELCOME .CHT │ TITLE    │ New Employee
      2          │ OVERVIEW.CHT │ BULLET   │ Tactile Toys, Inc.
      3          │ 90PROD  .CHT │ PIE      │ 1990 Sales by Product Line
      4          │ REGIONS .CHT │ BAR/LINE │ Regional Sales by Product Line
      5          │ ORGCHART.CHT │ ORG      │ Tactile Toys
      6          │ ORGCHART.CHT │

 Show description: New Employee Presentation

 F1-Help
                                                           F10-Continue
```

Figure 13.2: The EMP- SHOW slide show list

Although a chart name is listed next to 6, it has not been selected; you will notice that the type and description are not filled in like the other files. This chart will not be part of the final list.

5.   Press F10 when you are finished. The Slide Show Menu is displayed.

Displaying the Slide Show

Selecting a show file

Before you can view a slide show, the show file must be currently active. If you just created the show, it is automatically active. If you want to view a show you created at another time, you must first select (activate) it with the *Select slide show* option on the Slide Show Menu.

Screen-Show

To view a *ScreenShow* (Harvard Graphics' term for an on-screen slide show presentation), you choose the *Display ScreenShow* option on the Slide Show Menu. Harvard Graphics will then present the charts one at a time, in the order specified in the show list. Unless you specify otherwise, the slide show is presented in a manual mode, requiring you to press a key to view each chart. You can automate the presentation, however. The section on special effects tells you how.

When viewing a slide show in manual mode, do not use the spacebar to view the next slide. The spacebar will pause the show until you press another key.

Adding Special Effects

Now the fun begins! The special effects that Harvard Graphics offers for slide shows allow you to create lively and professional presentations. Some of these effects let you define the *transitions* between slides: how the slide is drawn on the screen and how the slide is erased from the screen. For example, you can gradually "fade in" and "fade out" the slide, or open the slide up like a blossoming flower. Though you have the opportunity to go wild here, be careful—you don't want to make your audience dizzy!

Transitions and Directions

Eleven transitions are available: Replace, Overlay, Wipe, Scroll, Fade, Weave, Open, Close, Blinds, Iris, and Rain. You can also select the direction the slide moves on and off the screen: Left, Right, Up, Down, In, or Out. Not all directions are applicable to all transitions, however. The best way to visualize these effects is to experiment with them.

Harvard Graphics does not support special effects on a VGA monitor. To see the transitions and directions on a VGA monitor, you must change the default screen to EGA. (From the Main Menu, choose *Setup* and then *Screen.*)

Let's take a look at the ScreenShow Effects screen. From the Slide Show Menu, choose option 3, *Add ScreenShow effects*. This screen lists the file names for the charts in your show and provides empty columns for you to enter desired special effects. The *Draw* and *Dir* columns contain the transition and direction for drawing the chart on the screen. The last two columns, *Erase* and *Dir,* contain the transition and direction for erasing the chart. The *Time* column will be discussed later.

*Screen-
Show
Effects
screen*

Notice that the row above your file name list is titled *Default.* In this row you can enter default transitions and directions. The defaults are used whenever you don't fill in a value for these effects on a specific chart.

*Default
values*

If you don't have time to enter specific transition/direction values for a slide show, enter your favorite effects in the *Default* row. These values will then automatically be used for all slides.

Define the special effects for your slide show. Start with the ScreenShow Effects menu displayed.

1. Move the cursor to the *Draw* column in the WELCOME.CHT row.

2. Press F6 to display a list of transition choices.

3. Highlight the *Fade* option and press Enter.

4. Tab to the next column, *Dir.*

5. Press F6 to display a list of directions.

6. Highlight the *Down* option and press Enter.

7. Refer to Figure 13.3 and complete the special effects for your show. Remember, press F6 to display a list of choices.

```
╭─────────────────────────────────────────────────────────────────╮
│                         Screenshow Effects                        │
│  ┌──────────────────────────────────────────────────────────────┐ │
│  │  Filename  │  Type   │  Draw  │  Dir  │ Time │ Erase │  Dir   │ │
│  ├──────────────────────────────────────────────────────────────┤ │
│  │  Default           │        │ Replace │     │      │        │  │
│  │ 1 WELCOME .CHT  │ TITLE    │ Fade   │ Down  │      │ Scroll │ Left  │
│  │ 2 OVERVIEW.CHT  │ BULLET   │ Scroll │ Right │      │ Iris   │ Out   │
│  │ 3 90PROD  .CHT  │ PIE      │ Iris   │ In    │      │ Wipe   │ Up    │
│  │ 4 REGIONS .CHT  │ BAR/LINE │ Wipe   │ Down  │      │ Open   │ Left  │
│  │ 5 ORGCHART.CHT  │ ORG      │ Close  │ Up    │      │ Rain   │       │
│  │                                                                │
│  └──────────────────────────────────────────────────────────────┘ │
│  F1-Help                                                           │
│  F2-Preview show        F6-Choices      F8-HyperShow   F10-Continue│
╰─────────────────────────────────────────────────────────────────╯
```

Figure 13.3: Choosing special effects for your slides

Instead of selecting effects from the F6-Choices list, you can type the first letter of the effect's name (for example, **S** for Scroll) in the ScreenShow Effects screen columns. As soon as you move the cursor, the name of the effect fills in. If several effects begin with the same letter, type the first two letters of the effect you want.

View your slide show with the new effects you added.

1. Move the cursor anywhere in the row for the first slide, WELCOME.CHT.

2. Press F2, and watch the first slide gradually appear on the screen, with the Fade effect.

3. Press any key. The Scroll Left effect causes the first slide to disappear, and the second slide then glides onto the screen, through the Scroll Right effect.

4. Continue pressing any key to view the rest of slide show.

Automating the Show

To make a self-running slide show, you can enter values in the *Time* column of the ScreenShow Effects screen. Each slide will display for the specified amount of time, and subsequent slides will automatically appear—without your having to press a key. Enter the delay time value in the format *mm:ss,* where *mm* is minutes and *ss* is seconds.

If, during the presentation, you want to display a slide for less time than you have programmed, you can press any key to override the time delay and move the show along. For additional time, press the spacebar to pause the slide show.

Editing a Slide Show

Once you have created a slide show, it is likely that you will want to modify the show list in some way. Using the *Edit slide show* option on the Slide Show Menu, you can add, delete, and move charts within the list. Table 13.1 lists the editing keys.

Key	*Description*
Tab	Move cursor between file list, show list, and show description
Ctrl-Del	Delete a chart
Ctrl-↑/↓	Move a chart up or down in the list

Table 13.1: Slide Show Editing Keys

Printing

If your purpose for creating a slide show is to batch print a group of charts, you'll need to do the following:

- Create a slide show of the charts you want to print.
- Make sure this slide show is selected. You may need to invoke *Select slide show* on the Slide Show Menu.
- Choose *Produce output* on the Main Menu.
- Select one of the following: *Print slide show, Plot slide show,* or *Record slide show.*

Printing the show list

To print your show list, choose option **9**, *Print slide show list,* on the Produce Output menu. This report details the order of your charts, their file names, types, and descriptions.

Step 14

Draw/Annotate

The Draw/Annotate option is a free-form drawing program included with Harvard Graphics. With this option, you can enhance your charts with additional text, lines, shapes, and clip art. For example, you may want to explain an unusually high or low data point on a bar/line chart. Or perhaps you want to draw a box around a title. You have the freedom of placing the supplemental text and graphics *anywhere* on the chart. The Draw/Annotate feature gives you the opportunity to be creative.

In Step 14 you will use the Draw/Annotate option to annotate a data point on the high/low/close chart you created in Step 11. The annotated chart is shown in Figure 14.1. In this simple example you will learn how to add text, circles, and arrows with Draw/Annotate.

Although you can use either the mouse or the keyboard to draw shapes, the mouse is faster and more convenient. Mouse users can simply point and click. Keyboard users must tap the arrow keys repeatedly and press Enter—it's a bit cumbersome.

Mouse

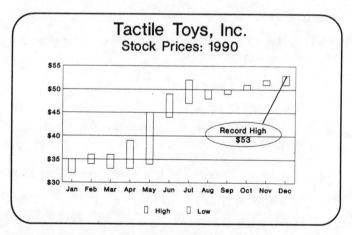

Figure 14.1: A chart annotated with Draw/Annotate

Beginning to Draw

You can use the Draw/Annotate feature to create new charts or to enhance existing ones. To annotate an existing chart, you must retrieve it before using the Draw/Annotate option. To design a chart from scratch, create a free-form text chart and then choose the Draw/Annotate feature.

To go directly into Draw/Annotate from a chart data form, press Ctrl-R.

Let's retrieve the STOCK90 high/low/close chart and supplement it with the Draw/Annotate option.

1. Get the STOCK90 chart.

2. Press Esc until the Main Menu is displayed.

3. Choose option **3**, *Draw/Annotate,* to begin drawing.

Your current chart appears inside a *chart box* on the right side of the Draw/Annotate screen, and the Draw menu is displayed on the left.

Adding Text

With Draw/Annotate you do not type text directly on the chart. Instead, you follow these three basic steps:

•   Specify options, such as text size and attributes.

•   Type a single line of text.

•   Use the mouse or arrow keys to position the text on the chart.

Add two lines of text to your STOCK90 high/low/close chart.

1. Choose option **1**, *Add.*

2. Choose option **1**, *Text.*

A box of options displays on the left. An input line, labeled *Text:*, appears at the bottom. Before you enter and position the text on the chart, you should specify text size and attributes. If you forget to change these options, the defaults will be used.

You cannot change the content, size, or attribute of text once you have placed it. You have to delete it using the *Delete* option on the Draw menu, and then add it again in the format you want.

3. Press F8 to move the cursor into the Text Options box.

4. Next to *Size,* type **3.5.**

5. Press F8 to return to the text line.

6. Next to *Text:* at the bottom of the screen, type **Record High** and press Enter.

A rectangular box appears on the screen. The size of this box corresponds to the amount of space needed for the text you entered. You will next position this box in the spot where you want the text to display on the chart.

7. Refer to Figure 14.1 for the text placement. Use the arrow keys to position the box, and press Enter when you are ready. Mouse users can move the mouse until the box is correctly positioned, and then press the left mouse button.

The text now appears on the chart. Notice that the bottom of the screen is still prompting you for text.

8. Type **$53** and press Enter. The rectangular placement box is automatically centered under the ''Record High'' line you just added.

9. As Figure 14.1 shows, this location is exactly where you want it. Press Enter to place the text.

10. Press Esc to return to the Add menu.

Drawing a Circle

To draw a circle with Draw/Annotate, you need to give Harvard Graphics two pieces of information: the circle's center, and the circle's size. Let's draw a circle around the text you just typed. (Actually, as shown in Figure 14.1, you'll draw an ellipse, not a circle. An ellipse is one of the circle options.)

Make sure the Add menu is still displayed from the previous exercise.

1. Choose option **5**, *Circle.*

2. Press F8 to move the cursor into the Circle Options box.

3. Press the spacebar to choose the *Ellipse* shape.

4. Move the cursor to the *Fill* option, and press the spacebar to turn it off.

If you don't turn off the Fill option, Harvard will automatically fill the circle with a color. The shaded circle will thus overlay and hide your text. If this happens, delete the circle and begin again, with *Fill* turned off.

5. Press F8 to draw.

A small cross now appears on your screen. This cross is officially called your *cross-hairs target.* It is like a cursor—it moves around the screen as you press the arrow keys or move the mouse. The bottom of the screen says "Select circle center."

6. Move the cross in between the two lines of text you added. This will be the center of the ellipse.

7. Press Enter or click the left mouse button.

8. Now you need to indicate the size of the circle. Press ↓ and → (or slide the mouse) until the text is completely enclosed in the box that appears as you move the cursor. The box will be replaced with a circle as soon as you press Enter.

9. Press Enter or click the left mouse button. Your ellipse should look like the one in Figure 14.1.

10. Press Esc to return to the Add menu.

Creating an Arrow

To create an arrow, you tell Harvard Graphics you want to draw a line, and then specify an option for the arrow direction. If you choose a left-pointing arrow, you mark the arrowhead first and then draw a line to the tail; for a right-pointing arrow, you mark the tail and then draw a line to the arrowhead.

With the Add menu still displayed, follow these steps to draw an arrow on your chart:

1. Choose option **4**, *Line.*

2. Press F8 to change the options.

3. Press the spacebar until the right-pointing arrow is selected.

4. Next to *Width,* type **1.5**.

The default line width, 5.5, creates a thick, heavy line. In most cases, you will want to choose a narrower width. To change the default options, press F8 from the main Draw menu.

5. Press F8 to draw.

6. Refer to Figure 14.1 for the placement of the arrow. Notice the message "Enter to add point" at the bottom of the screen. To add the point, move the cross-hairs target to the circle's edge, and press Enter or click the left mouse button.

7. Now, as you move the cross, a line stretches from the first point to the cross. Move the cross up to the top of December's high/low bar (see Figure 14.1) and press Enter or click the mouse. The arrow is now drawn.

8. Press Esc until the Main Menu is displayed.

9. Save your chart with the same name.

Draw/Annotate or Draw Partner?

Draw/Annotate is one of two drawing utilities included with Harvard Graphics 2.3. The second utility, called *Draw Partner,* is a separate program that is accessed from the Applications menu (F3). The two drawing utilitites have similar capabilities, but Draw Partner offers a wider variety of shapes and a number of advanced features. Draw/Annotate, however, has the advantage of being directly integrated with Harvard Graphics and is consequently more accessible.

Draw Partner is a separate product with its own set of menus and options, and is beyond the scope of this book.

Step 15

Symbols

In Step 14 you learned how to enhance your charts with the drawing tools included in the Draw/Annotate feature. Here in Step 15 you will learn another way of making your charts more interesting: with *symbols*. Symbols are simple drawings that are sometimes called *clip art*. Harvard Graphics comes with over 500 different symbols—maps, animals, people, vehicles, and buildings, to name a few. For a complete list, refer to the Symbols booklet included with your Harvard Graphics software. By using symbols in your charts, you don't have to be an artist to add that professional graphics touch.

Symbol Files

Related symbols are grouped together in files that have the .SYM extension. For example, pictures of animals are stored in ANIMALS.SYM.

When you installed Harvard Graphics, you had an opportunity to copy the symbol files. If you did install these files, they were stored in a directory called SYMBOLS, a subdirectory of your Harvard Graphics program directory. If you didn't copy the symbols, you need to use the INSTALL program to do it now—so that you can do the exercises in this Step. If you are short on disk space, you don't have to copy all the symbol files; you only need ANIMALS.SYM. Refer to Step 1 for information on installation.

Adding a Symbol to a Chart

To add a symbol to an existing chart, you first retrieve the chart and then call up the Draw/Annotate screen. You select a symbol file and choose a symbol from the list of samples on the screen. (Figure 15.1 displays all the symbols available in the ANIMALS.SYM file.) Finally, you indicate where you want to place the symbol in your chart.

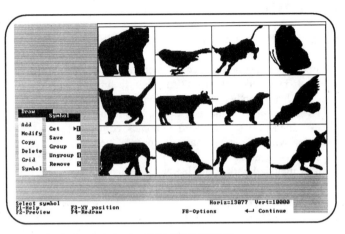

Figure 15.1: Symbols in the ANIMALS.SYM file

In this exercise you will add a picture of a stuffed animal to the opening slide of the presentation to new employees. Figure 15.2 illustrates the chart with a kangaroo symbol at the bottom.

1. Get the WELCOME title chart.

2. From the Main Menu, choose option **3**, *Draw/Annotate*.

3. Choose option **6**, *Symbol*.

4. Choose option **1**, *Get*.

A list of files in the SYMBOLS directory appears. If no files are listed, either your .SYM files are in a different subdirectory, or you didn't install the symbol files.

5. Choose ANIMALS.SYM.

One by one, each of the symbols in the ANIMALS file is drawn on the screen, enclosed in a separate box. To choose a symbol, move the cross-hairs target anywhere inside the symbol's box, and press Enter or click the left mouse button.

New Employee
Orientation Program

Welcome to
Tactile Toys, Inc.

Figure 15.2: A text chart with a symbol added

6. Use the arrow keys or mouse to move the cross-hairs to the kangaroo.

7. Press Enter or click the left mouse button.

A box now appears in the middle of the screen. This box represents the size and placement of the symbol. If you press Enter now, the symbol drops down onto the middle of the chart. However, unless you are placing the symbol in an empty chart, you will probably want to reposition the box.

8. Press the backspace key; this lets you determine a new position for the upper-left corner of the box. The box disappears, and the cross-hairs target is displayed. The message "Select first box corner" appears at the bottom of the screen.

9. As shown in Figure 15.2, the kangaroo will go underneath "Tactile Toys, Inc." So, move the cross slightly below the *c* in "Tactile." Press Enter or click the left mouse button to set the upper-left corner.

10. Your next task is to specify the lower-right corner of the symbol—this process will determine the size of the

symbol. Move the cross-hairs target to the right and down until the box is approximately the size of the symbol shown in Figure 15.2. The lower-right corner should line up with the *I* in "Inc." Press Enter or click the left mouse button.

The box is now replaced with the kangaroo symbol. If you have a monochrome monitor, the symbol appears as a solid shape on the screen, but in the printed chart you will be able to clearly see the kangaroo's features (arms, legs, eyes, and ears). If you save the file, the kangaroo symbol will be part of the WELCOME.CHT title chart file. Whenever you draw or print this chart, you will see the kangaroo.

Repositioning a Symbol

Frequently after you add a symbol, you will discover that its size or position is not quite right. The Modify option on the Draw menu lets you change the size or placement of any graphics element (lines, circles, rectangles, symbols, and so forth) that you have added to a chart.

*Selecting
an object*

Whether you are moving, sizing, copying, or deleting an object in your chart, you need to tell Harvard Graphics which particular object you want to modify. This process is called *selecting*. When you are prompted to select an object, you simply move the cross-hairs target anywhere in the middle of the object, and press Enter or click the left mouse button. At that point, you will see small squares appear in the extreme four corners of the object. If this is the object you want to modify, select the option *Choose this* at the bottom of the screen. Otherwise, choose *Select next* or *Retry.*

In this next exercise, let's assume you didn't place the symbol in its ideal location. You want to move the kangaroo so that it is centered on the page.

1. From the Draw menu, choose option **2**, *Modify.*

2. Choose option **1**, *Move.* The message "Select object" appears at the bottom of the screen.

3. Move the cross to the middle of the kangaroo.

4. Press Enter or click the mouse. Small squares appear in the four corners around the kangaroo, indicating you have selected this object.

5. To confirm your selection, press Enter to select *Choose this.*

6. Use the mouse or the arrow keys to center the kangaroo. As you press the arrow keys or move the mouse, the box moves, but the kangaroo remains stationary. Don't worry—as soon as you confirm the position, the kangaroo hops into place.

7. Press Enter or click the left mouse button to complete the move.

8. Press Esc to return to the Main Menu, and save the file.

For more precise placement of objects, you can display a grid of dots in the chart box. The grid helps you align objects, but it does not print. *Grid* is an option on the Draw menu.

Other Symbol Options

The Symbol menu contains several other options in addition to the *Get* option you used earlier in this Step. Here are brief explanations of the other options.

With the *Save* option, you can create your own symbols for use in any chart. For example, you can use Draw/Annotate to create a design out of various shapes, text, and symbols, and then save the entire group of objects as a single symbol.

Creating your own symbols

The *Group* option allows you to modify multiple objects as if they were one symbol. For example, in Step 14 you created an ellipse with text inside it. To move both objects (text and circle) at once, you can first group them together, and then use the Move command. Without the *Group* option, you would have to move the ellipse and text in two separate steps.

Modifying multiple objects

*Removing
an object*

The *Remove* option on the Symbol menu permanently deletes a symbol from the .SYM file. If all you want to do is remove the symbol from your chart, do not use the *Remove* option; use the *Delete* option on the Draw menu.

Macros

If you find that you are giving the same commands over and over again in Harvard Graphics, consider creating some macros. *Macros* automate your use of the program by allowing you to press a couple keys to issue an unlimited number of keystrokes and commands. Macros are similar to the speed keys you learned in Step 2. For example, instead of choosing *Produce output* from the Main Menu and then *Printer* to go to the Print Chart Options screen, you can print with the speed key Ctrl-P.

Here are a few ideas for macros you may want to create:

Macro ideas

- Get a specific symbol (such as a company logo)
- Type your company name
- Print a chart with specific options
- Retrieve a chart you update freqently

Loading the Macro Program

The macro feature is not actually built into Harvard Graphics—it is a separate, memory-resident program that can be used while you are in Harvard Graphics. You must have at least 500K of available RAM before you can load both the MACRO program *and* the Harvard software.

Because this program is separate from Harvard, you load it from the DOS prompt before you load Harvard. The MACRO.COM program file is located in your Harvard Graphics directory.

Load the MACRO program.

1. If necessary, exit from Harvard Graphics.

2. Change to the Harvard Graphics directory. For example, if your directory is named HG, type

   CD \HG

   and press Enter.

3. To load the macro program, type

   MACRO

   and press Enter. A message appears on the screen indicating that you can invoke the Macro menu by pressing Alt-zero. Wait to do this until you have loaded Harvard.

4. To load Harvard Graphics, type

   HG

   and press Enter.

The MACRO program remains in memory until you turn off or reboot your computer. You can even use MACRO in other software packages, such as Lotus 1-2-3. Keep in mind that you will need to load MACRO each time you want to use or create macros. If you are going to use MACRO regularly, you will want to create a DOS batch file that loads MACRO.COM before loading Harvard Graphics.

Unloading MACRO

If you want to free up memory (about 60K) for other programs or projects, you can unload the MACRO program. To do this, you'll need to

- Exit Harvard Graphics.

- At the DOS prompt, press Alt-zero.

- On the Macro menu, select *Unload MACRO*.

Recording a Macro

Creating a macro is similar to recording a message on your answering machine, or recording a song on a tape recorder. Here are the basic steps:

- Set the stage. Do whatever needs to be done before you start recording—retrieve a file, display the appropriate menu, place the cursor, and so on. (These are the actions that need to take place *before* your macro executes its actions.)

- Turn on the macro recorder.

- Type the keystrokes to be recorded. (These are the actions your macro will execute.)

- Turn off the macro recorder.

Keep the following rules in mind when you are recording a macro:

Rules for recording

- You cannot record mouse movements or mouse button clicks.

- Once you turn on the recorder, *everything* is recorded—even mistakes.

- When recording a selection from a menu, *type* the letter or number next to the option. Do *not* use the arrow keys to highlight the option, because the next time you run the macro, a different option might be chosen.

- When changing an option that has several choices, do *not* use the spacebar to move the marker. Instead, *type* the first letter or number of the option.

The macro you create in this Step will specify a few options (a double border and the Roman font) before printing a chart.

Prior to turning on the macro recorder, you should retrieve a chart. If you turn on the recorder before getting the chart, this chart retrieval action will be recorded in the macro. We want the macro to work with *any* chart, not just this one.

1. Get one of your charts.

2. Press Esc until the Main Menu is displayed.

3. Press Alt-zero to display the Macro menu. (You must use the zero on the top row of the keyboard—the zero on the ten-key pad won't work.)

4. Choose *Record a macro.* You are prompted for a file name.

5. Type **1** for the macro name, and press Enter. The recorder is now turned on and you are ready to begin recording keystrokes.

Macro names

Each macro is stored in its own file with the extension .MAC. The file name can be up to eight characters long, but the fastest way to "play back" a macro is to assign it a one-character name (A–Z, 1–9). These *one-key macros* are executed by pressing the Alt key with the one-character letter or number.

Now let's record the keystrokes for this macro.

1. Press F8 to display the current chart options.

2. Press Enter to move the cursor to the *Border* option.

3. Type **D** for *Double.*

4. Press Enter to move the cursor to the *Font* option.

5. Type **R** for *Roman.*

6. Press F10 to continue.

7. Type **6** to choose *Produce output.*

8. Type **1** to choose *Printer.*

9. Press F10 to begin printing. The current chart prints.

Turning off the recorder

10. To turn off the recorder, press Alt-zero to display the Macro menu, and select *Stop recording macro.*

Your screen does not indicate whether you have the macro recorder turned on or off. *Don't forget to turn off the macro recorder after the last keystroke you want recorded.* If you forget, every single key you type or press will be recorded in the macro until you finally do turn off the recorder.

Playing Back a Macro

After recording a macro, always play it back to make sure it recorded properly. There are two ways to execute a macro, depending on how you named it during the recording process. One way to run a macro is to choose *Play back a macro* on the Macro menu, and type the macro name.

One-key macros

If the macro has a one-character name, you can execute it by pressing Alt with that letter or number. As you can see, one-key macros are the quickest way to inititate macro playback and execution.

Use the macro you just recorded to print another chart.

1. Get another chart. (You don't need to save the previous chart.)

2. Press Esc until the Main Menu is displayed.

3. Press Alt-1 to play back the macro. As the commands are executed, you see menus quickly flash on the screen. Macros execute the commands much faster than you can.

If you discover a mistake in the macro, or if you accidentally execute the wrong macro, you can cancel the playback by pressing Alt-End.

Troubleshooting .

If nothing happens when you execute your macro, check the following:

• Is MACRO loaded?

• Did you type the correct macro name and directory?

- If it's a one-key macro, is it located in the current macro directory? (To change the current directory, use the *Change macro directory* command on the Macro menu.)

If your macro doesn't work properly, you have two options to try and rectify the problem. First, try recording the macro again. Remember not to use the arrow keys to highlight menu selections—this could be the source of the problem. Instead, type the letters and numbers that correspond to the options you want to select.

Another method for correcting a macro is to bring the .MAC file into a text editor or a word processor that can edit text files. The .MAC file contains cryptic keystroke codes, however, and can be somewhat difficult to decipher.

Step 17

Templates and Chartbooks

15

After you have used Harvard Graphics for a while, you may discover that you frequently use the same combination of options for a certain chart type. For example, most of your bar charts may have the Overlap 3D effect with a shadow box around the legends. Or perhaps the text in your simple lists is usually sized at 4.5, aligned on the left, and indented 20. Instead of having to specify these settings each time you create a chart that uses them, you can permanently modify the default settings by creating a chart *template*. A template is a file that contains the settings you use most often. Like the macros you learned about in Step 16, templates eliminate repetitive tasks.

Templates not only save you time, but also promote consistency in presentations that have many charts. For example, if you need to make 20 simple-list text charts for a presentation, you will want the style (text size, placement, and attributes) to be the same in all 20 charts. A template can help insure this consistency.

Creating a Template

To create a template, you begin by creating a chart in the usual manner. If you have an existing chart that already has the settings you want to store in the template, you can get this chart.

What kind of things can you store in a template?

- Current chart options—orientation, border, font, and palette (F8 from the Main Menu)
- Text size and placement settings (F7)
- Attributes (F5)
- Options and titles (F8 from the chart data form)

- Symbols and other graphic elements added with the Draw/Annotate feature or the Draw Partner application

- Specific chart data (optional)

As you set your template options, you may want to enter dummy data, so that you can view an example of the chart type you are creating. Then, when you save the template, you can tell Harvard Graphics to clear out these values.

Titles, subtitles, and footnotes are automatically stored with all types of templates except for text chart templates. However, you can get titles into text chart templates by specifying No to the *Clear values* option when you save the template. Just make sure you delete any unwanted lines of text *before* choosing this option.

In this exercise you will create a template for the settings you use most often in pie charts.

1. Create a Pie chart.

2. Press F8 to display the first options page.

3. Next to *Subtitle,* type **Tactile Toys, Inc.**

4. Turn on the *3D effect* option.

5. Press PgDn to display the next options page.

6. Turn off the *Show value* option.

7. Turn on the *Show percent* option.

8. Press F10 to return to the Main Menu.

Saving a Template

The Get/Save/Remove menu offers special options for saving and getting templates. The *Save template* option saves the file with a .TPL extension.

Template names

There are two types of names you can assign to templates. If you want to permanently change the default settings for a certain chart type, give the template one of the names listed in Table 17.1.

When a template with any of these names exists, Harvard retrieves and uses it automatically whenever you create a chart. For example, if a template called TITLE.TPL exists, Harvard uses it every time you create a title chart. These templates are called *default style templates.*

File Name	Chart Type
TITLE	Title chart (Text)
LIST	Simple list (Text)
BULLET	Bullet list (Text)
2_COLUMN	Two-column (Text)
3_COLUMN	Three-column (Text)
FREEFORM	Free-form (Text)
PIE	Pie
BARLINE	Bar/Line
AREA	Area
HLC	High/Low/Close
ORG	Organization
MULTIPLE	Multiple charts

Table 17.1: Template Names for Default Style Templates

On the other hand, when you are creating templates for a special project, you should assign unique, descriptive names to your template files; use names other than the ones listed in Table 17.1. These templates must be manually retrieved whenever you want to use them—they are not automatic. See "Using a Template" in this Step for additional information.

Save the pie template you just created, as a "permanent" default style template.

1. From the Main Menu, choose option **4**, *Get/Save/Remove.*

2. Choose option **4**, *Save template.*

3. Next to *Template name,* type **PIE**.

*Clearing/
saving the
values*

Take a look at the special options offered on the Save Template screen. The default for the *Clear values* option is Yes. If you leave the default at Yes, any text or values you have entered while creating the template will *not* be stored in the template. (The one exception is the chart's title, subtitle, and footnote; this text is stored regardless of whether you select Yes or No for this option.) If you change *Clear values* to No, all data and settings are stored in the template.

*Import
data link*

If you initially created the current chart by importing data from another file (Lotus 1-2-3, ASCII, or Excel), you can create a link between the template and the specific file from which you imported. Refer to Steps 18 and 19 for a thorough discussion of importing data.

Pay close attention to your choice of directory for storing your templates. When you create a new chart, Harvard Graphics looks in the *current directory* for any default style templates and retrieves the appropriate template if it's there. If a default style template is not in the current directory, no template is used; Harvard does not check other directories. Thus, if you save PIE.TPL in C:\HG, and later create a pie chart in C:\HG\CHARTS, the PIE template will not be retrieved automatically. One way of circumventing this problem is to copy the template into each of your chart directories.

If the *Save template* screen is still displayed, press F10 now to continue. Press Enter to confirm the clearing of the data values.

Using a Template

How you use a template depends on the name you assigned to it. Default style templates are easy to use: They are retrieved automatically. For example, whenever you create a pie chart from the directory in which you saved PIE.TPL, the new default settings and titles will be entered for you automatically.

If you assigned a unique name to your template, you must retrieve the template instead of creating a new chart. When you get the template, all the settings are automatically in place for the designated chart type, and you are ready to enter data. To retrieve a template, use the *Get template* option on the Get/Save/Remove menu. Select the template that you want. The chart data form is then displayed and you can proceed as usual. (If you chose *not* to clear the data values when you saved the template, the data form displays the data that's in the template.) Use the *Save chart* option to save the file after you enter data; the file is saved with a .CHT extension.

Getting a template

You can also use the *Get template* option to modify an existing template. Then use *Save template* to save your changes.

Creating a Chartbook

If you create many different templates, you may begin to have difficulty keeping track of them all. That's why *chartbooks* were invented. A chartbook is similar to a DOS subdirectory, in that both are named storage compartments that hold related files. For example, you can create a chartbook named BARS for all your bar chart templates. A chartbook is actually a disk file (with the extension .CBK) that contains a list of templates.

To create a chartbook, you'll need to

- Choose option **8**, *Chartbook menu,* from the Main Menu.

- Choose option **1**, *Create chartbook.*

- Enter a directory, name, and description. The directory must be the one in which the templates are stored.

- Press F10.

- From the displayed list, select the template file names you want included in the chartbook.

- Press F10 when you are finished.

Using a Chartbook

Once your chartbooks are created, you can use them to help you retrieve your templates. When you wish to create a chart with a template from a chartbook, you follow these basic step:

- Select the chartbook that contains the templates you want to use. *Select chartbook* is an option on the Chartbook Menu.

- Choose *Create chart* on the Chartbook menu. This option displays a list of templates stored in the current chartbook.

- Highlight the template you want to use, and press Enter or click the mouse. The chart data form for this template will then be displayed.

You can designate a default chartbook as one of the Harvard Graphics default settings. The chartbook you specify as the default will be selected automatically for each work session. You won't need to choose the *Select chartbook* option unless you want to use a different chartbook.

To set up a default chartbook, choose *Setup* from the Main Menu, and then choose *Defaults*. Next to *Default chartbook,* enter the chartbook name. This chartbook must be in the default data directory; you cannot enter a path before the file name.

Step 18

Importing/Exporting Data

No one lives in a vacuum, not even a dedicated Harvard Graphics user. Sooner or later you are probably going to need to transfer files back and forth between Harvard and other software programs. For example, the data you want to graph in Harvard may have already been typed in a word processor or spreadsheet program. Rather than retyping it in Harvard, you can import the data. Likewise, you may want to include a Harvard Graphics chart with other text on the same page of a report.

The Import/Export option on the Main Menu is your gateway to data transfer. This Step covers how to import ASCII data into text and graph charts and also how to export a Harvard Graphics chart to an external program. Step 19 concentrates on importing spreadsheet data.

Importing ASCII Text

ASCII is a standard file format that contains only text and no special formatting codes; it is recognized by virtually every software program. ASCII was developed so that data could easily be used among different programs. Text typed in your word processor must be converted to ASCII before you can bring it into Harvard Graphics.

There are several circumstances in which you may need to bring data from an ASCII file into a text chart. Perhaps you or someone else has already typed the chart text in a word processing program, unaware that the charts need to be printed in Harvard Graphics. Or the files may have been created before Harvard was purchased. You may prefer to type rough drafts of your text charts in your word processor, to take full advantage of editing features—such as cut and paste—that are not available in Harvard. All of these situations call for interchanging ASCII data between programs.

Preparing the ASCII File

Since each word processor has a different method for creating ASCII files, consult your word processor's documentation if you aren't already familiar with the procedure. Here are a few rules to keep in mind when typing chart text in your word processor.

- The first line of the file becomes the chart's title.

- Do not bother formatting the text with bold or underline attributes, or with different fonts, because this formatting is removed when you create the ASCII file.

- The maximum number of lines that can be imported is 48.

Creating the Text Chart

Importing ASCII text files is a simple and easy process. You'll follow these basic steps:

- From the Main Menu, choose option **5**, *Import/Export*.

- Choose option **3**, *Import ASCII data*.

- If necessary, press F3 to change to a different directory.

- Select the desired file name from the list.

The first part of the file is displayed in a window. Notice that each line is numbered, and a ruler appears at the bottom of the window. These numbers help you identify the length and the width of the file.

Import settings

- If necessary, change any import settings.

When importing an ASCII file into a text chart, you will want to leave most of the default chart settings in Harvard as they are. The one option you might need to change is the *Read from column... to column* setting. The *to column* value should correspond to the maximum number of characters on lines of the ASCII file. Using Ctrl with the arrow keys, you can scroll through the file and check the line lengths. If they exceed the *to column* value (the default is 60), the text will be truncated in the Harvard file. Be sure to increase this value if necessary.

- Press F10.

The text will then be displayed in a free-form text chart. At this point, you can format the text, and save and print the chart as you normally would.

Imported text is automatically entered into a free-form chart data form, but you are not stuck with this chart type. After the text is imported, you can bring the data into a different chart type. Just create a new chart of the appropriate type, and then answer Yes to the *Keep current data* question. The text from the free-form chart is transferred into the new chart's data form.

Changing the chart type

Importing Delimited ASCII Data

Another type of ASCII file contains *delimiters* in addition to text. A delimiter is a character that separates spreadsheet columns or database fields. When a database file is stored in ASCII, you can separate each field with a tab or comma. Likewise, when you store a spreadsheet file in ASCII, you can use the tabs or commas as column delimiters. Frequently, quotation marks are used as delimiters around fields containing text.

Preparing the Delimited File

If the data you want to graph is currently stored in a database or statistical package, you can output the data into a delimited ASCII file and then bring it into Harvard Graphics. If you aren't sure how to create a delimited file in your database or statistical program, refer to the software's documentation. When you have a choice of delimiters, use

- Commas to separate fields
- Quotes to surround text fields

- Carriage return/line feeds between each record (thereby placing each record on a separate line)

These delimiters are Harvard Graphics' default settings.

You need to know the file's delimiters before you can import the data. Use the DOS TYPE command to view the file if you don't know what delimiters are used. This command was used to display the file in Figure 18.1.

Creating the Graph

You can import the delimited ASCII data into any Harvard chart type you like. Before you use the Import/Export option to do this, you should create a chart of the desired type and then return to the Main Menu. When you don't specify a chart type before you import the data, the data is automatically entered in a free-form text chart.

Follow these basic steps to import the delimited ASCII file:

- From the Main Menu, choose option **5**, *Import/Export.*

- Choose option **4**, *Import delimited ASCII.*

```
C:\WORKS>TYPE FIG18-1.TXT
"North-East",950,600,170,130
"South-East",990,200,100,240
"Mid-West",850,500,330,180
"North-West",450,400,220,150
"South-West",360,700,400,200

C:\WORKS>
```

Figure 18.1: A delimited ASCII file displayed with the DOS TYPE command.

- If necessary, press F3 to change to a different directory.

- Select the desired file name from the list.

- If necessary, change the delimiters.

In the ASCII Delimiters dialog box, the *Quote character* delimiter is the symbol used at the beginning and end of text fields; the quotation mark is the default. The *End of field delimiter* is the symbol placed between fields. Although a comma is the default, some programs delimit fields with tabs. To specify a tab delimiter, use #9 (9 is the ASCII code for the tab character). The *End of record delimiter* indicates how each record is separated. The default codes, #13#10, are the ASCII codes for carriage return and line feed.

Delimiters

- Press F10.

- When prompted with

      Import first record as series legends

  choose Yes if the column headings or field names are included in the ASCII file. Choose No if the first row contains the first record of data.

The data form for the chart type you previously specified is displayed next. You can then draw the chart, change options, edit and save it, or do whatever you like to the chart.

Exporting Harvard Graphics Charts

If you want to include a Harvard Graphics chart in a word processed or desktop published report, you first need to convert the chart into a standard format the other programs understand. Harvard Graphics can export to the following formats:

- Professional Write word processor

- Encapsulated PostScript

- Hewlett-Packard Graphic Language (HPGL)

- CGM Metafile

Consult your word processing or desktop publishing program documentation for eligible formats to import.

CGM
Metafiles

Before you can export to CGM Metafile format, you must use the INSTALL program to install VDI device files for Metafiles. Also, you must include the following lines in your CONFIG.SYS file:

```
device=C:\HG\VDI\META.SYS
device=C:\HG\VDI\GSSCGI.SYS
```

First, retrieve the chart you want to export. Then you'll need to do the following:

- From the Main Menu, choose option **5,** *Import/Export.*

- Choose option **8,** *Export picture,* or option **9,** *Export CGM metafile.*

- Enter a file name for the exported picture. Use the file name extension .EPS for Encapsulated PostScript files, and .CGM for Metafiles.

- On the Export Metafile menu, tell the program you want to use Harvard Graphics fonts (select Yes) or standard Metafile fonts (select No). Choosing Harvard Graphics fonts creates a file three times the size of a file with Metafile fonts, but you get a chart that contains the exact fonts you saw in the Harvard chart.

- When exporting other picture files, choose a *Picture quality* (Standard or High) and a Format (Professional Write, Encapsulated PostScript, or HPGL). The High quality option creates a file two to three times the size of Standard quality.

- Press F10.

This converted Harvard Graphics file can now be imported into PageMaker, Ventura Publisher, WordPerfect, or another program that accepts the file format you chose. Refer to the appropriate program documentation for details on importing the various file formats.

Importing Spreadsheets

If the data you want to graph with Harvard Graphics is stored in a spreadsheet file, you don't need to reenter it in Harvard; nor do you need to convert the file to ASCII. Harvard Graphics can directly access data in Lotus 1-2-3 and Excel files. If you use a spreadsheet program other than 1-2-3 or Excel, you still may be able to import the data. Check your spreadsheet program's documentation to see if files can be saved in 1-2-3 or Excel format.

Why would you want to use Harvard Graphics to create charts of your spreadsheet data if the spreadsheet program itself has built-in graphing capability? The answer to this question is immediately apparent by comparing Figures 19.1 and 19.2. Figure 19.1 is a Lotus 1-2-3 graph, and Figure 19.2 is a Harvard Graphics chart of the same data. You can see that graphs created in spreadsheet programs are clearly inferior to those created in a dedicated graphics program like Harvard. More options are available, and the output

*Spread-
sheet
charts vs.
Harvard
Graphics
charts*

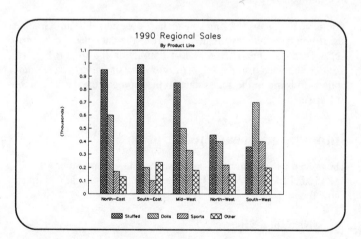

Figure 19.1: A Lotus 1-2-3 graph

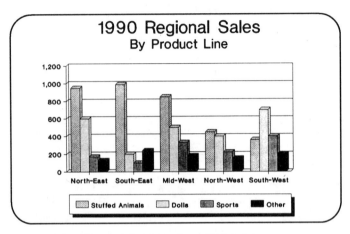

Figure 19.2: A Harvard Graphics chart of 1-2-3 data

quality is much higher. Many users like to create the basic graph in their spreadsheet program and then import it into Harvard for fine-tuning and printing.

You have two ways to bring spreadsheet data into Harvard Graphics. If you have already created a chart of the data, use the *Import Lotus graph* or *Import Excel chart* options on the Import/Export menu. Otherwise, use the *Import Lotus data* or *Import Excel data* options to bring in the series data so that you can create the graph in Harvard.

Importing Spreadsheet Data

The procedure for importing spreadsheet data—from either a 1-2-3 or an Excel file—is similar. In order to bring in the data, you must know the

- Name of the file
- Subdirectory in which the file is stored
- Cell addresses or range names of the titles, x-axis data, and each series

Write down this information while you are in Lotus 1-2-3 or Excel, and/or print the spreadsheet with the column letters and row numbers.

Before you import the data, you need to create a chart, because Harvard Graphics inserts the imported data into the current data form. For example, if you want a bar chart, create a Bar/Line chart and then return to the Main Menu.

Create a chart first

Note: Rather than returning to the Main Menu, you can directly import spreadsheet data into a chart data form by pressing Ctrl-L (for Lotus 1-2-3) or Crtl-X (for Excel).

From the Main Menu, follow these basic steps to import your 1-2-3 or Excel data:

- On the Main Menu, choose option **5**, *Import/Export.*

- Choose option **2** to *Import Lotus data,* or option **6** to *Import Excel data.*

- Press F3 to change to the directory containing your spreadsheet.

To specify a default directory from which you will import spreadsheets, go to the Setup Defaults screen and enter your Lotus 1-2-3 or Excel data directory next to *Import directory.*

- Harvard next displays a list of files in the current directory that have the extensions .WKS, .WK1, and .WK3 (Lotus) or .XLS (Excel). Highlight the name of the file you want and press Enter.

Even though Harvard Graphics displays .WK3 files on the import list, 1-2-3 Release 3 files cannot be imported. To import a Release 3 file, you must save the file in 1-2-3 with a .WK1 extension.

- Fill in the Harvard import data form.

Figure 19.3 displays a completed import data form for a 1-2-3 file. Notice "\A1" and "\A2" next to *Title* and *Subtitle*. These codes

```
                        Import Lotus Data
        Worksheet name: STEP19   .WK1

                Title: \A1
             Subtitle: \A2
             Footnote:

                       Legend          |    Data Range

          X | X axis data              | A6..A10

          1 | Stuffed Animals          | B6..B10
          2 | Dolls                    | C6..C10
          3 | Sports                   | D6..D10
          4 | Other                    | E6..E10
          5 | Series 5                 |
          6 | Series 6                 |
          7 | Series 7                 |
          8 | Series 8                 |

            Append data:  ►Yes    No

  F1-Help         F3-Select files
                  F4-Clear ranges F6-Range names           F10-Continue
```

Figure 19.3: Import data form for a Lotus 1-2-3 file

indicate that the two titles are entered in cells A1 and A2 of the spreadsheet. (Alternatively, you can type in the titles yourself. Enter the appropriate range addresses or range names in the *Data Range* column.) You can also type the legends (Stuffed Animals, Dolls, and so forth) in the *Legend* column, or you can wait until the data is imported.

To view a list of range names in the current spreadsheet file, press F6 in the *Data Range* column. You can then select a name from the list.

Once you have filled in the import data form, press F10 to display the data in the Harvard chart data form. You can now press F2 to view the chart, or F8 to begin specifying options.

Importing Spreadsheet Charts

Bringing in a basic chart you have created in Lotus 1-2-3 or Excel is even easier than bringing in the raw data, because you don't need to specify the data ranges. You just need to know the name of the graph. Excel creates each graph in a separate file with the extension .XLC. Lotus 1-2-3 stores its graphs within the spreadsheet file. If you have multiple graphs within a spreadsheet file, be sure to assign each one a unique name.

Unlike the process of importing data, when importing a graph you do not need to first create a chart. This is because the chart type is defined in the imported graph. Follow these steps to import a Lotus 1-2-3 or Excel chart:

- From the Main Menu, choose option **5**, *Import/Export*.

- Choose option **1** to *Import Lotus graph*, or option **5** to *Import Excel chart*.

- Press F3 to change to the directory containing your spreadsheet.

- Harvard Graphics now displays a list of files from the current directory that have the extensions .WKS and .WK1 (Lotus) or .XLC (Excel). Highlight the name of the file you want, and press Enter.

- If you are importing a 1-2-3 graph, you must supply an additional piece of information: the graph name. Harvard displays a list of the graphs you saved with 1-2-3's /Range Name Create command. Choose the name of the graph to import, or if you didn't name the graph, choose the name MAIN (the default graph name).

- In response to the *Import data only* question, choose No to import both the chart *and* its data. Choose Yes to import *only* the data.

The imported chart will now display on the screen. You can choose *Enter/Edit chart* on the Main Menu to view the data and set the options.

Three powerful features included with Harvard Graphics are Spell Check, Calculate, and the color palettes.

- *Spell Check,* like the spelling checker you probably use in your word processing program, finds typos and spelling errors and suggests possible correct spellings. Spell Check works in any chart type, not just text charts.

- The *Calculate* feature gives you much of the power of your spreadsheet program. Within Harvard, you can enter formulas, use built-in functions, and modify the arrangement of your data series.

- The *color palette* feature lets you manipulate the colors used on your screen and on color output devices.

Spell Check

To run the spelling checker, retrieve your chart and press F4 from the Main Menu. The spelling checker then compares each word in your chart with the program's on-disk dictionary. If the word is not found in the dictionary, Harvard Graphics will highlight the word and give you a list of options. Figure 20.1 shows the misspelled word "Sysstems." As you can see from the menu in the figure, you have several choices.

If the highlighted word is correctly spelled after all, choose *Word ok, continue* or *Add to dictionary.* The first option skips over the word and goes on to the next misspelled word. If you think you will use the word frequently in other charts, consider adding the word to the Spell Check dictionary. That way, next time Harvard Graphics will not think the word is misspelled.

Adding words to the dictionary

For real typos and spelling mistakes, choose *Type correction* and edit the misspelled word, or select one of the suggested words.

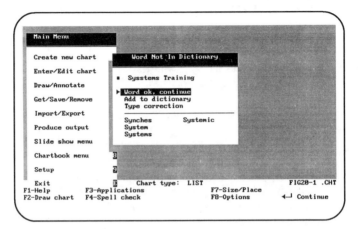

Figure 20.1: Spell Check finds the word "Sysstems" misspelled

*Other uses
for Spell
Check*

Spell Check actually does more than identify spelling errors. It also looks for the following types of mistakes:

- Incorrect capitalization

- Incorrect punctuation

- Repeated words

Spell Check does not find all spelling errors. For example, some text, though mistyped, is actually a word—such as "I *red* the book." Harvard Graphics will not identify this as a mistake. To be safe, you will still need to proofread your charts.

Calculate

There are a number of ways you can use the Calculate feature. First, you can do on-the-fly calculations for a single data point. For example, if a data point is the sum of several values, you can use Calculate—instead of a calculator—to perform the calculation *and* enter the answer. Another use for Calculate is to compute all the data points in a series. For example, you can divide two series to create a third series. Another way to use Calculate is for editing your data. There are options for deleting, copying, and moving columns of data.

Here are the basic steps for calculating:

- In the chart data form, move the cursor to the data point or series to be calculated. When performing a calculation on an entire series, you can place the cursor anywhere in the column.
- Press the Calculate key, F6.
- You are prompted for a legend name. When creating a new series, you should enter an identifying column heading here. For example, if the column calculates a moving average, **Moving Average** could be the legend.
- Type your formula next to *Calculation.* (You will get a chance to practice a few formulas in the following exercises.)
- Press Enter or F10 to complete the calculation.

Making a calculation

In this exercise, you will perform a simple calculation in one of your chart data forms.

1. Get the chart named REGIONS.
2. Move the cursor to "850" in the Stuffed Animals column.
3. Press F6.
4. Move the cursor next to *Calculation.*
5. Type **125+450+325**.
6. Press Enter. The former value (850) is replaced with the newly calculated value (900).

Table 20.1 lists the calculating functions, and Table 20.2 lists the editing functions. The #*n* in each function name refers to the series (column) number. For example, to average the first series, use @AVG(#1).

Function	Description
@AVG(#n,#n)	Averages the values in up to seven different specified series.
@CUM(#n)	Calculates cumulative totals of series #n.
@DIFF(#n)	Calculates the difference between each adjacent value in series #n.
@MAVG(#n)	Calculates the moving average of series #n.
@MAX(#n,#n...)	Computes the maximum value in each row of up to seven different specified series.
@MIN(#n,#n...)	Computes the minimum value in each row of up to seven different specified series.
@PCT(#n)	Divides each value in series #n by the total of series #n to compute a percentage value.
@RECALC	Recalulates the formulas in all series after a value has been changed.
@REXP(#n)	Computes exponential regression curve of series #n.
@RLIN(#n)	Computes linear regression curve of series #n.
@RLOG(#n)	Computes logarithmic regression curve of series #n.
@RPWR(#n)	Computes power regression curve of series #n.
@SUM(#n,#n...)	Adds the values in up to seven different specified series.

Table 20.1: Calculating Functions

Function	Description
@CLR	Erases data in current series.
@COPY(*#n*)	Copies series *#n* to the current column.
@DUP(*#n*)	Duplicates series *#n* to the current column. Creates a permanent link between the original and duplicated series.
@EXCH(*#n*)	Exchanges data in current series with series *#n*.
@MOVE(*#n*)	Moves series *#n* to the current column.
@REDUC	Sorts and combines duplicate x-axis labels.

Table 20.2: Editing Functions

Next, let's create a calculated series in the US-INTNL line chart. This new series will subtract series 2 from series 1.

1. Get US-INTNL.

2. Place the cursor anywhere in the empty series 3 column.

3. Press F6 to Calculate.

4. Next to *Legend,* type **Difference**.

5. Next to *Calculation,* type **#1–#2**. This formula subtracts series 2 from series 1.

6. Press Enter.

The subtraction formula is automatically applied to the entire column. The values in your screen's *Difference* column should match Figure 20.2. Notice the diamond next to the *Difference* heading. This symbol indicates the column is the result of a calculation.

Create a second new series that averages series 1 and 2.

1. Place the cursor anywhere in the empty series 4 column.

2. Press F6 to Calculate.

3. Next to *Legend,* type **Average**.

```
┌──────────────────────────────────────────────────────────────────┐
│                      Bar/Line Chart Data                           │
│  Title: U.S. and International Sales                               │
│  Subtitle: Tactile Toys, Inc.                                      │
│  Footnote:                                                          │
│                                                                    │
│              X Axis      │ United │ Internatio │◆Difference │◆ Average│
│     Pt       Year        │ States │    nal     │            │        │
│                                                                    │
│     1   1985             │  0.5   │    0.1     │   0.4      │  0.3   │
│     2   1986             │  0.9   │    0.2     │   0.7      │  0.55  │
│     3   1987             │  1.7   │    0.7     │   1        │  1.2   │
│     4   1988             │  3.2   │    1.1     │   2.1      │  2.15  │
│     5   1989             │  5.6   │    1.9     │   3.7      │  3.75  │
│     6   1990             │  8.1   │    2.3     │   5.8      │  5.2   │
│     7                    │        │            │            │        │
│     8                    │        │            │            │        │
│     9                    │        │            │            │        │
│    10                    │        │            │            │        │
│    11                    │        │            │            │        │
│    12                    │        │            │            │        │
│                                                                    │
│  F1-Help        F3-Save        F5-Set X type              F9-More series│
│  F2-Draw chart  F4-Draw/Annot  F6-Calculate   F8-Options  F10-Continue  │
└──────────────────────────────────────────────────────────────────┘
```

Figure 20.2: Series 3 and 4 (Difference and Average) are calculated columns

4. Next to *Calculation,* type **@AVG(#1,#2)**. This formula averages the values in series 1 and 2.

5. Press Enter.

The averages fill in the series 4 column. Check your results against Figure 20.2.

Color Palettes

If you have a color monitor and/or a color output device (printer, plotter, or film recorder), you can use the *color palette* feature to modify the colors used in your charts. The color palette defines what colors are used for the different areas of the chart. For example, the chart background is one color, each series is a unique color, and the chart titles use yet another color. If the colors used don't appeal to you, you can choose a different palette or modify the existing colors in your current palette.

Screen and output palettes

Your color palette actually has two parts to it: the *screen palette* controls what colors you see on the screen, and the *output palette* specifies the colors used on a color output device. When possible, the screen colors match the output colors, so that you can get a good screen representation of how the chart will look when printed, plotted, or recorded. Both palettes are stored in a single file.

For users who do not have a color output device, your color selection controls only what colors you see on your screen; the colors are ignored when you print. If you have a color printer, such as the Hewlett-Packard PaintJet, these color selections also determine what colors are printed. If you are using a plotter or a film recorder, you will want to select a palette that is designed for your output device. The default palette works with a Polaroid film recorder.

Selecting a Palette

Each chart can have its own color palette. This section tells you how to use the predefined color palettes that are included with Harvard Graphics.

In the following exercise, you will determine which color palette your current chart is using, and then select a different palette.

1. First, press F2 to display the current chart (US-INTNL). Make a note of the colors used in each of the four series.

2. Press F8 from the Main Menu to display the Current Chart Options screen. The current palette (hc23) is indicated at the bottom of this screen. This palette is the default.

3. From the Main Menu, select option **9**, *Setup*.

4. Choose option **7**, *Color palette*.

5. Choose option **3**, *Select palette*.

A list of palettes—files that have a .PAL extension—is displayed. (If no palette files display, you are probably not in the Harvard Graphics program directory. Press F3 to change to a different directory.) As mentioned previously, the default palette is HG23.PAL. This palette is set up to work with an EGA monitor and a Polaroid film recorder. Also included with Harvard Graphics

Palette (.PAL) files

are palette files for the different color output devices it supports. For example, PLOT6PEN.PAL contains the color palette for a six-pen plotter.

6. Let's try a palette that has a greater variety of colors than HG23.PAL. Highlight HG.PAL and press Enter.

7. Press Esc to return to the Main Menu, and then F2 to draw the chart with the new color palette. Look at the colors you noted for the default palette, and compare them with the colors now used. Which do you prefer?

The palette you just selected only applies to the current chart (US-INTNL). When you save the chart, the palette will be permanently recorded in the file. Thus, every time you retrieve US-INTNL, it will use the HG.PAL color palette. Save the chart now with the same name.

Default palette

To change the default palette used in any future charts you create, select the *Defaults* option on the *Setup* menu. Next to *Default palette* on the Default Settings screen, type the name of the palette file. You do not need to type the .PAL extension. This change in the default does not affect the charts you have already created.

To change the palette used in any existing charts, you have two options. After getting the chart, you can use the *Select palette* option, as you did in the previous exercise. The second way to specify a palette is to enter the palette name next to *Palette file* in the Current Chart Options screen (press F8 from the Main Menu). Use the first method if you are not sure of the palette file name. Otherwise, it's quicker to specify the palette with the second method.

Modifying a Color Palette

To see what colors are used in a palette, and then change these colors, you use the *Edit palette* option on the Palette screen. Let's do this now.

1. From the Main Menu, select option **9**, *Setup*.

2. Choose option **7**, *Color palette*.

3. Choose option **2**, *Edit palette.*

The Color Palette Setup screen now appears, as shown in Figure 20.3. At first glance, this screen is somewhat intimidating, with all of its cryptic numeric codes. The first column is the easiest part of the screen to decipher—it describes each of the sixteen colors in the palette. We will ignore the other columns for now.

4. To see the palette colors, press F2.

Looking at the colors

The numbered pie slices in the upper-left corner of the screen correspond to the sixteen colors in the palette. The remainder of the screen shows you examples of how a pie, bar, and text chart will look in this palette. Press any key now to return to the Color Palette Setup screen.

Notice that three of the columns on this screen are labeled *Screen,* and the final three columns are titled *Output.* These column titles refer to the two parts of the palette file. Each color is created by

Mixing your own colors

```
                          Color Palette Setup
   Palette file: HG        Screen: EGA              Output: AGX SERVICE
                           Red    Green  Blue       Red    Green  Blue
    1   White             1000   1000   1000       1000   1000   1000
    2   Cyan                 0   1000   1000          0   1000   1000
    3   Magenta           1000      0   1000       1000      0   1000
    4   Green                0   1000      0          0   1000      0
    5   Blue                 0      0    660          0      0    850
    6   Red               1000      0    330       1000      0    330
    7   Yellow            1000   1000    330       1000   1000    330
    8   Orange            1000    330      0       1000    330      0
    9   Royal Blue           0      0   1000        150    150   1000
   10   Gold              1000    660      0       1000    660      0
   11   Violet             660      0    660        660      0    660
   12   Pink              1000      0    660       1000      0    660
   13   Grey               660    660    660        660    660    660
   14   Crimson            660      0      0        660      0      0
   15   Dark Green           0    330      0          0    330      0
   16   Black                0      0      0          0      0      0

   Background color: 16    Description: HG.PAL default palette for HG 2.1

   F1-Help
   F2-Show palette                                          F10-Continue
```

Figure 20.3: The Color Palette Setup screen

mixing together a certain amount of red, green, and blue. Thus, this screen indicates the mixture used for each of the sixteen colors. Fortunately, Harvard comes with these mixtures predefined for you. If you are feeling bold, though, you can create your own colors by changing the mixtures of red, green, and blue.

Be careful when experimenting with the colors in a color palette, because there is no way to undo or cancel your changes; the palette is saved automatically when you leave the Color Palette Setup screen. Therefore, rather than editing a palette directly, make a copy of it first with the *Create palette* option on the Palette menu. The new palette will have the same colors as the currently selected palette. You can then experiment freely without worry.

Index